"How Christians live with  is one of the great questions of our day s resource to help move toward right ar

John Ortberg, senior pasto _to Go_

"_From Bubble to Bridge_ arriv ...ne. When fear and mistrust have grown in our national politics, we need to develop our understandings of each other in Christian love. Through these personal, thoughtful, and well-written essays, Larson and Shady have given us just what we need to grow our ethic of love across religious boundaries."

Brian Howell, professor of anthropology, Wheaton College, author of
Short Term Mission

"Religious conflicts often dominate today's headlines, and Christian colleges are faced with the challenge of preparing students to live faithfully and graciously as followers of Jesus in a world where peace and good will among people of differing faiths is desperately needed. _From Bubble to Bridge_ explains what's at stake, analyzes the difficulties, and maps a positive path forward. Engaging, well-organized, and overflowing with practical wisdom, this is the guide to interfaith relations that evangelical educators have been seeking."

Douglas Jacobsen and Rhonda Hustedt Jacobsen, codirectors, Religion in the Academy Project

"_From Bubble to Bridge_ is an exceptional resource for an important task facing the church today. Larson and Shady describe with clarity the present landscape—one in which people of different faiths (or of no specific faith) live and work together, side by side. For this multifaith world, the authors provide resources to think Christianly about interfaith dialogue and to live hospitably across difference. They are masters at bridging thoughtful theoretical work with practical suggestions and exercises drawn from their significant experience in leading students at a Christian university along these paths. _From Bubble to Bridge_ is essential reading for Christian educators, pastors, and other leaders committed to Jesus' call to love both God and neighbor."

Jeannine K. Brown, professor of New Testament, Bethel Seminary, San Diego

"Marion Larson and Sara Shady offer an inspiring, informative, and practical guidebook for Christians seeking to navigate a world where contact between people of different religious faiths is rapidly increasing. They focus in particular on students living in the bubble-like existence of Christian colleges and suggest that these students have the potential to become interfaith bridge builders. Therefore, our future needs this book as required reading at all Christian colleges."

Curtiss Paul DeYoung, executive director, Community Renewal Society, Chicago, author of _Living Faith_

"We live in a divided world where difference often leads to hostility and violence. Many times religion is at the heart of these divisions. *From Bubble to Bridge* is a thoughtful, field-tested approach that moves students and faculty from distance and distrust to engagement and hospitality with religious neighbors. Rather than losing their faith and understanding, students can become more confident in their own commitments while engaging peers from other faith traditions. Professors Larson and Shady write out of their own conviction, passion, and experience. It is hard to imagine a more thoughtful, practical resource in addressing the challenging issues of today's multifaith world."

Jay Barnes, president, Bethel University

"In this well-researched book, authors Larson and Shady articulate why Christians should foster life together across multiple faith traditions. Their ideas are a bridge from biblical teaching and foundational Christian convictions to effective interfaith practices. Their suggestions can aid faculty, staff, and students in fostering a healthy campus climate and productive community engagement. This book was written for such a time as this."

Shirley J. Roels, director, Network for Vocation in Undergraduate Education, Council of Independent Colleges

"Because most of us are not likely to know much about the actual views of our religious neighbors, we too often live in fear of those who are different from us. At any moment of the day, we can see that our world is full of violence, hateful words and actions, prejudice, injustice, and oppression that are rooted in fear and ignorance regarding our religious neighbors. At the same time, we also glimpse individuals who are living peacefully with their religious neighbors and are speaking and acting in ways to support those neighbors, near and far. This book compels us to ask and act upon our answer to the question, what does it look like to act from love rather than fear when interacting with our religious neighbors? As a starting place for this work, Marion H. Larson and Sara L. H. Shady remind us of the biblical mandate to love God and to love our neighbors as ourselves. They have been the catalysts on our own campus for understanding what it means to love our religious neighbors. May this book inspire others to live in ways that promote the common good in our world."

Debra K. Harless, provost, Bethel University

From Bubble to Bridge

Educating Christians for a Multifaith World

MARION H. LARSON
SARA L. H. SHADY

FOREWORD BY EBOO PATEL

IVP Academic

An imprint of InterVarsity Press
Downers Grove, Illinois

InterVarsity Press
P.O. Box 1400, Downers Grove, IL 60515-1426
ivpress.com
email@ivpress.com

InterVarsity Press® is the book-publishing division of InterVarsity Christian Fellowship/USA®, a movement of students and faculty active on campus at hundreds of universities, colleges, and schools of nursing in the United States of America, and a member movement of the International Fellowship of Evangelical Students. For information about local and regional activities, visit intervarsity.org.

Cover design: Faceout Studio
Interior design: Beth McGill

ISBN 978-0-8308-5156-0 (print)
ISBN 978-0-8308-9155-9 (digital)

Printed in the United States of America ♾

 As a member of the Green Press Initiative, InterVarsity Press is committed to protecting the environment and to the responsible use of natural resources. To learn more, visit greenpressinitiative.org.

Library of Congress Cataloging-in-Publication Data

Names: Larson, Marion H., 1960- editor.
Title: From bubble to bridge : educating Christians for a multifaith world /
  [edited by] Marion H. Larson and Sara L. H. Shady ; foreword by Eboo Patel.
Description: Downers Grove : InterVarsity Press, 2016. | Includes
  bibliographical references and index.
Identifiers: LCCN 2016041794 (print) | LCCN 2016044524 (ebook) | ISBN
  9780830851560 (pbk. : alk. paper) | ISBN 9780830891559 (eBook)
Subjects: LCSH: Christianity and other religions.
Classification: LCC BR127 .F755 2016 (print) | LCC BR127 (ebook) | DDC
  261.2—dc23
LC record available at https://lccn.loc.gov/2016041794

P	20	19	18	17	16	15	14	13	12	11	10	9	8	7	6	5	4	3	2	1
Y	33	32	31	30	29	28	27	26	25	24	23	22	21	20	19	18	17	16		

For Erin, Evan, Gavin, and Minty

Contents

Foreword

Eboo Patel

The final weeks of 2015 were difficult for American Muslims. High-profile terrorist attacks in Paris and San Bernardino, California, strengthened the connection between Islam and violence in the public imagination. Certain presidential candidates played on fears of Muslims to score political points. There was even debate about whether the United States should bar all Muslim immigrants from entering. To many, it felt like religious prejudice was being legitimized at the highest levels of American public discourse.

Dr. Larycia Hawkins, an associate professor of political science at Wheaton College, watched these developments with dismay. She had long taught her students that theoretical solidarity with the marginalized was insufficient. The Christian faith and the example of Jesus demanded what she called "embodied solidarity." The Advent season in 2015 gave her the opportunity to illustrate.

Claiming a theological responsibility to demonstrate sisterhood with Muslims suffering discrimination, Hawkins donned a Muslim headscarf and wrote on her Facebook page that Muslims and Christians "worship the same God." The administration at Wheaton, maintaining that Hawkins's statement crossed a doctrinal line, suspended her. The case generated enormous controversy, both within the evangelical community and in the broader public. Evangelical theologians such as Miroslav Volf and David Gushee weighed in. Wheaton students and faculty publicly took sides. The *Washington Post*, CNN, and the *New York Times* covered the story, and the *Chicago Tribune* reported every twist and turn. Ultimately, the Wheaton administration and Professor Hawkins agreed to amicably part ways, but everyone knew that the issues raised by the "Doc Hawk" case were here to stay.

There was a time not so long ago when the interfaith solidarities of a Wheaton College professor would have barely made the newspaper in Wheaton itself. We live in a very different era. Such issues are now in the front of many people's minds and increasingly at the center of their faith lives. Undoubtedly this has something to do with the charged role that religious diversity issues play in our public discourse, and also the fact that interfaith interaction is now the rule rather than the exception. People look at situations like the one that unfolded at Wheaton College, place themselves in the story, and ask, "What would I do?"

From Bubble to Bridge has arrived at the perfect time. The authors shed light rather than heat on the question of how evangelical Christian colleges ought to engage religious diversity. They manage to take evangelical theology, Christian education, and other religions seriously—no mean feat! They are honest about the fact that evangelical colleges were designed to insulate and, while maintaining that there is value in faith-alike spaces, they fully recognize that such institutions can no longer pretend that their bubbles continue to be hermetically sealed. Diversity creeps in through friendships, news stories, civic encounters, social movements, and the like. Larson and Shady show, in a manner that is both intellectually compelling and practically useful, that evangelical colleges can be leaders in interfaith bridge-building.

It is impossible to overstate the importance of this work. I have been involved with the organized interfaith movement for twenty years now, fifteen of those as founder and president of Interfaith Youth Core. In my experience, the single most challenging group to involve in interfaith efforts is the evangelical Christian community. Too often, interfaith leaders view the entire evangelical world through the narrow prism of high-profile polarizers like Pat Robertson and Jerry Falwell. And too often, evangelicals decline invitations to participate in interfaith initiatives, stating that even stepping through the door requires them to dilute their faith commitments.

The sad irony is that interfaith engagement is meant to dispel such myths and fears. But it can't work unless people are willing to take the risk to build the bridge and to cross it. This book goes a long way toward achieving that end.

The fact is, there is no returning to the hermetically sealed bubble. All of us are required to respond to diversity; the question is how we will do that. A single glance at religion-related news illustrates that the anti-bridge-building forces are strong. Engaging with this reality is one of the great challenges of our century, one with profound implications for both faith identity and civic harmony. Simply put, if we are unable to use the materials of our traditions to fashion the bridges of interfaith cooperation, we forfeit the territory to people who would fashion from that same material barriers of division or bludgeons of destruction.

Acknowledgments

There are countless people to thank for their roles in inspiring and supporting our work.

To our Bethel colleagues, thank you for charting new territory with us. Thank you, President Jay Barnes and Provost Deb Harless, for your deep commitment to interfaith engagement at our institution and beyond. Thank you, Amy Poppinga, for teaching us how to do this work well, for friendship and encouragement, and for continuing conversations on campus, off campus, and up in Alexandria. Thank you to the many Bethel colleagues who partner with us in promoting interfaith work in our bubble and across many bridges. Thank you to current and former students for learning along with us. And, to our former colleagues, Leon Rodrigues and Curtiss DeYoung, thank you for sitting in a room with us several years ago and helping us to courageously build our first year of interfaith projects.

To our partners at Interfaith Youth Core, thank you for your enthusiastic support of our work and consistent commitment to broadening Christian involvement in the interfaith movement. Eboo Patel, thank you for beginning this movement and helping all of us imagine a better world. Katie Bringman Baxter and Joe Morrow, thank you for your investment in our campus and helping us learn how to grow an interfaith movement in the context of an evangelical Christian university. Cassie Meyer and Noah Silverman, thank you for your continued support of faculty development. Amber Hacker, thank you for pouring so much creative energy into this project, helping us think about promoting this work to multiple audiences, and generating the idea of using narratives from those involved in interfaith work.

To those who generously shared your personal stories, thank you for illustrating the good work that is done when we courageously leave the bubble for the bridge. Thank you, Tanden, Janna, Greg, Amber, April, Rachael, Ola, Amy, and Anna.

To David Congdon and the rest of the staff at IVP Academic, thank you for your support of this project and multiple suggestions for strengthening it.

To Jamie and the rest of the staff at the Bad Waitress, thank you for the good coffee, food, and service at our Thursday morning writing meetings. You even care enough to bring the coffee to the table before we order it and ask us how the book is coming along.

And, most importantly, to our families, thank you for helping us make time for writing and cheering us on along the way.

Out of the Bubble

On an autumn evening, we gathered in a local mosque with several students from our Christian university. We were there to participate in an interfaith dialogue series sponsored by the St. Paul Interfaith Network. This five-week series, titled "My Truth and Your Truth: Absolutes and Openness in Our Religious Traditions," included a series of presentations by local religious leaders followed by a question-answer time and then small-group discussions facilitated by a team of volunteers. Some students were attending these dialogues as part of a Social and Political Philosophy class. The class, taught by Sara Shady, required us to reflect on the role of religion in society, and attending the dialogues provided real encounters with religious diversity. Other students were there with Marion Larson, attending the dialogues as part of a first-year honors class in which she required her students to learn about a faith tradition different from their own.

The topic of discussion that evening was a particularly sensitive one: conversion. The Christian representative on the panel advocated a contextual view of missions that acknowledged God's many means of self-revelation—including in religions other than Christianity. This speaker said a person could come to be a faithful

Christ-follower without leaving behind all she had known and valued in her home culture and even her home religion. This position alone challenged many of our students, who worried that the speaker was compromising too much of the gospel in his efforts to respect other cultures and religions. But then the representatives of other faith traditions began to express in strong terms that they were deeply offended by this Christian panelist because he made it clear that, ultimately, Christ is *the* way and *the* truth. Several of our students were shocked and confused. They weren't sure whether to feel angry and defensive or guilty and ashamed.

This event drew all of us into some serious reflection. Should the presenter have censored his views out of respect for those in attendance? Is it possible to talk about something such as evangelism without incurring deep offense? How do we genuinely listen to and respect those who have different religious beliefs while retaining commitment to our own?

How do we genuinely listen to and respect those who have different religious beliefs while retaining commitment to our own?

While many of our students had come along that evening to earn credit for an assignment, a few were drawn to the event simply out of curiosity. For most of them this was a completely new experience. Like many college students, our students tend to form relationships with those who are most like themselves in terms of race, ethnicity, and class—and also in terms of religion. This tendency is compounded at our Christian university, where the Christian faith is central to much that we do and talk about, both in and out of the classroom. But most of our students don't have many opportunities to talk about their faith with people who believe differently, and they haven't yet learned to listen well when those who aren't Christians share about their own faith. In fact, for many of our students, simply walking into a mosque or talking with a Jewish person or meeting a person from the Baha'i faith—which most of them didn't even know existed—is a radically stretching experience. On this particular night the discussion not only broadened their horizons; it deeply shook their assumptions about what it means to be a Christian.

So why involve students in these types of events? Because we believe there's unfathomable value in helping Christians learn to constructively navigate a world of increasing religious diversity. The premise of this book is that Christians who seek to live and serve graciously in a religiously diverse world must also deliberately and thoughtfully engage with our religious neighbors. We firmly believe that not only is such engagement in line with God's command that we love all of our neighbors, including those who believe differently; it also helps us to develop a mature, committed faith that's at the same time humble and open to learning from others.

OF BUBBLES AND BRIDGES

We've spent most of our lives learning and working in "bubbles," a common term used to describe the relatively homogenous culture of many evangelical Christian college campus communities. As students, Larson spent four years inside the "Wheaton bubble," Shady within the "Taylor bubble." Now we've worked together for several years inside the "Bethel bubble." Bubbles don't exist only around Christian college campuses, however. Whether we're involved in a club or an organization, a classroom or dormitory or church, bubbles form whenever we draw clear boundaries between "us" and "them" and focus most of our time and energy in the safety of "us."

From our experience, bubbles aren't entirely bad. But they're definitely limiting. Bubbles provide a relatively safe space for us to be ourselves, they help affirm and solidify our identities among others with similar beliefs, and they provide respite from the challenges of the world around us. But staying in bubbles doesn't prepare us for life in the twenty-first century. Life inside a bubble often fails to help us see the world from other perspectives, because it doesn't provide enough opportunity for building meaningful and constructive relationships with people who believe differently—the kind of relationships we'll need if we hope to face myriad global challenges.

Bubbles isolate. As Eboo Patel, founder and president of Interfaith Youth Core (IFYC), puts it, "Religion in the 21st century can be a bubble of isolation; a barrier of division; a bomb of destruction; or a bridge of cooperation."[1] Patel has described the challenge and opportunity of religious diversity in his book *Acts of Faith*. Mirroring W. E. B. DuBois's famous statement that "the problem of the twentieth century is the color line," Patel suggests that "the twenty-first century will be shaped by the question of the faith line."[2] In response to this challenge, we believe, along with Patel and many others, that we must leave our bubbles and build bridges of cooperation and collaboration that connect people of different faiths.[3]

For over a decade, a movement has been spreading across college campuses to inspire and engage students, faculty, and staff in this crucial work. A problem, however, is that many Christians (particularly evangelicals) aren't seen as bridge-builders. Although there are many different reasons for this, some of which are rooted in stereotypes and misunderstanding, we must accept the fact that society at large doesn't perceive Christians as being all that good at loving our neighbors, particularly when our neighbors belong to a different religious tradition. At almost every conference and workshop we've attended in the last ten years, the same questions are always raised: What should we do about the evangelicals? Why won't they play alongside everyone else in the proverbial sandbox? How can I get them to participate in the interfaith events on my campus? Why aren't evangelical student organizations promoting interfaith work?

A common goal of education, from a Christian perspective, is to cultivate a mature intellect and faith, one that enables us to lead lives of meaningful service as we actively engage and seek to transform the world. Over the years much has been written by Christian academics about the integration of faith and learning, and this scholarship continues to discuss the importance of helping students learn to weave together the academic, social, and spiritual aspects of their lives. Many recent works on Christian higher education have considered what faith-learning integration might look like in the twenty-first century; however, little attention is given to preparing Christian students to navigate a religiously diverse world. Christians need to be more intentional about preparing to love their neighbors, even (perhaps especially) when those neighbors have different religious beliefs. For those on evangelical Christian college campuses, such preparation needs to include interfaith service and dialogue on and off campus as an important aspect of education and spiritual development.

> **Christians need to be more intentional about preparing to love their neighbors, even (perhaps especially) when those neighbors have different religious beliefs.**

The type of interfaith engagement that we prescribe, and that's gaining momentum at hundreds of colleges and universities around the country, isn't about fostering theological relativism. We're not asking Christians to accept the beliefs of other religions as theological truth. Rather, we recognize that "while we all might pray in

separate mosques, churches, synagogues, and temples we still share
schools, stores, and streets"; thus, interfaith engagement is about
"improving these common social places and building understanding
between communities."[4] This is clearly consistent with the goal of
many Christians to be positive agents of transformation in the world.

RELIGION AND HIGHER EDUCATION

While higher education exists largely to help students develop intellectually and gain information they previously lacked, learning isn't
just a matter of acquiring subject matter. Instead, learning is both
cognitive and affective, involving the whole person. "Education
worthy of its name is essentially education of character," says Martin
Buber.[5] Among other things, this means that even if a student ac-
quires impressive amounts of information, true education hasn't
necessarily occurred.

Church-affiliated schools and organizations have long recognized
this. We're committed to holistic education. We see integration of
faith and learning as central to such an education, so faculty and staff
work hard to help students consider how their faith commitments
might influence their academic learning, as well as how their academic learning might affect their faith. We look for ways to help
students connect their experiences in the dorm or in service projects
or in chapel with their classroom learning, and vice versa.

As an example, consider the mission statement of the university
where we teach:

> Boldly informed and motivated by the Christian faith, Bethel
> University educates and energizes men and women for excel-
> lence in leadership, scholarship, and service.[6]

A common phrase used to describe Bethel's educational goal is that
we want to help students and ourselves "become whole and holy
persons," meaning that education must be simultaneously spiritual,

intellectual, and social. Similar missions are shared by Christian organizations working in the context of higher education. For example, InterVarsity Christian Fellowship's vision statement is "to see students and faculty transformed, campuses renewed, and world changers developed."[7]

Holistic education requires both "challenge and support" in order to promote learning, a recurring theme among much educational literature. "Challenge" nudges the learner into new territory, stretching her beyond her current way of thinking or acting. "Support" helps to encourage and motivate and reassure a learner that she's capable of meeting the challenge. This is true in faith development as well. Research shows that a prime factor in faith development is the sort of challenge that leads people to examine what they believe and why, along with the support needed for reflecting on what's been encountered.[8] For the most part, Christian colleges and universities and Christian organizations do a great job of supporting students in the development of a mature and informed faith. But do we provide enough challenge?

> **For the most part, Christian colleges and universities and Christian organizations do a great job of supporting students in the development of a mature and informed faith. But do we provide enough challenge?**

While students who attend church-affiliated schools and participate in Christian student organizations have many productive opportunities to develop their Christian faith, interactions with those from other religious traditions are often limited—particularly for students on campuses where virtually all students are professing Christians (and where most of those come from evangelical branches of Christianity). Students may emerge from such schools as fluent speakers of "Christian," but we also want to help our students become "theologically bilingual, to understand the God-language of another community, and to understand our own more clearly in the process."[9] Developing religious literacy across faith traditions involves following Warren Nord's advice to "take religion seriously," meaning that "religion is understood from the inside, studied in sufficient depth to make sense of it, treated as a live option in its most compelling forms."[10]

Within the context of Christian colleges and student organizations, we often meet Nord's goal when it comes to Christianity. But a relevant question for Christians to ask is: Are we taking other religions seriously as well? Not only is answering this question in the affirmative a matter of justice and equity, it's also essential for the intellectual, spiritual, and social development of Christian college students. In fact, extensive research on the degree to which college students exhibit a pluralistic orientation toward others—marked by a move from tolerance toward engagement, acceptance, and understanding of diverse worldviews—is lowest among evangelical Christian students.[11] We simply can't constructively engage and serve the world beyond the campus if we don't learn how to navigate religious diversity constructively, balancing religious commitment with hospitality and openness toward others. Based on years of experience and research, we've come to believe that the goal of holistic education can be met only through interactions with members of other faith traditions. Such interactions help to humanize "religious others," making dialogue and reconciliation possible, as well as encouraging reflection on one's own faith tradition and subsequent spiritual growth within that tradition.

A Path Forward

In the chapters that follow, you'll find a rationale for Christian involvement in interfaith engagement, a theoretical model for what healthy interfaith engagement might look like, and several practical ideas for moving forward in this important work on Christian college campuses and within Christian organizations.

In chapter one we focus specifically on the undeniable need for us to address the civic reality of religious pluralism around the globe. In many parts of today's world, immigration and globalization put people into contact who had previously remained separate. This poses new challenges that can lead to prejudice and even violence. To help counteract such realities, we need to be deliberate in developing networks of engagement between and among people who feel separated from each other—including those separated by religious belief and practice.

While some argue that we can avoid social friction by keeping religion out of civic life, we disagree. We support efforts to build a pluralistic society characterized by respect for and relationships with diverse neighbors. In supporting civic pluralism, however, we don't necessarily have to support theological pluralism. Thus, Christians can (and should) participate in efforts to promote civic pluralism, and Christian colleges and universities can be instrumental in preparing students for life in a religiously pluralistic society.

Chapter two builds on the civic imperative by arguing that Christians also have a faith-based responsibility to pursue interfaith cooperation. Following Jesus' teaching that the two most important commands are to love God and to love our neighbor, we explore what it means to love our religious neighbors, drawing from the long and rich tradition of Christian hospitality. This examination is assisted by Amy Oden's observation that hospitality consists of four "movements": prepare, welcome and restore, dwell, and send.[12] Each of these movements provides additional insights (and challenges) for Christians seeking to be loving neighbors to those from other faith traditions.

Spending time with our religious neighbors in a spirit of hospitality equips us to show love in additional ways. We explore what this looks like by suggesting that Christians take responsibility for the harm Christians have done to religious neighbors, intended or unintended; that we fight religious prejudice; and that we ensure that we're not guilty of bearing false witness when we speak about other religions. We ought to be guided by the Golden Rule, particularly when it comes to our efforts at evangelism. And we should seek to partner with our religious neighbors in promoting the common good.

But even though we know God asks us to love all people, we also know it can be difficult to build meaningful ongoing relationships with those who believe differently. Chapter three explores some of the primary reasons Christians are reluctant to join interfaith initiatives and uses biblical teachings to help urge us to participate. Christians may understand the civic and religious imperatives for interfaith engagement, but the first barrier we often face to being good religious neighbors is what Brian McLaren calls a "conflicted" Christian identity—one that wants to be strongly committed to Christ without being hostile to religious others but that also believes these are incompatible goals. The second barrier commonly faced is the social status ambiguity experienced or perceived by many American evangelicals. There are numerous examples of "Christian privilege" in our country, yet many evangelicals feel embattled and far from privileged. So they spend more time focusing on defending the faith than they do engaging persons from different traditions. These first two barriers often lead to a third—fear of our religious neighbors, a fear that can impede our ability to love.

What does it look like to act from love rather than fear when interacting with our religious neighbors? The parable of the lost son and the parable of the good Samaritan can provide useful guidance. We can be both strong, committed Christians and good religious neighbors.

Once Christians are ready to consider interfaith engagement, there are usually questions about what exactly this should look like. In particular, how do we hold on to our beliefs while trying to be hospitable toward those who believe differently? Chapter four addresses this question by providing a model for interfaith engagement rooted in the philosophy of Martin Buber and the theology of Miroslav Volf. There's a tendency to swing to one of two extremes when thinking about how to engage difference. At one extreme, we might aim for a mere tolerance of another's view. In this case we accept a person's right to hold a view different from our own, but we make no attempt to understand that view, let alone to build a meaningful relationship with the other person. At the other extreme we unreflectively accept the other's view. In this case, we affirm all that's good in another tradition and focus on reducing all traditions to their lowest common denominator of shared values. But in doing so we don't think critically about the strengths and weaknesses of differing views, including our own.

Instead of pursuing the extremes of mere tolerance or complete acceptance, we propose a third model for interreligious dialogue: inclusion. An inclusive model of dialogue recognizes and respects both interpersonal and intellectual boundaries, promoting a shared reality where all partners in the dialogue seek to understand each other's position, even if they don't entirely agree with it. In asking us how we can balance our own belief commitments with our responsibility to be open to and challenged by the other's perspective, Buber and Volf provide us with images and insight. When engaging in interfaith dialogue, we aren't asked to leave our beliefs at home. Nor are we asked to act as if differences between religions were immaterial. We are, however, asked to seek genuine, inclusive dialogue that fosters mutual understanding and opens the possibility for ongoing positive relationships.

In order to become the sort of people who are prepared for inclusive dialogue, we must develop certain character traits. Chapter five introduces three key virtues that we believe are necessary for constructive interfaith engagement: receptive humility, reflective commitment, and imaginative empathy. In this chapter we utilize the work of Catherine Cornille and Martha Nussbaum. Cornille's *The Im-Possibility of Interreligious Dialogue* (2008) explores qualities that make a person well-suited for interfaith engagement—including humility, commitment, and empathy. Her discussion of each quality is spacious, showing a range of ways in which each might be demonstrated. In addition, she shows how each might influence the other. Reflecting on this combination of characteristics can help us see the qualities that we hope to develop as well as some of the ways in which interfaith engagement might be challenging. Two emphases in Nussbaum's *Cultivating Humanity* (1997) and *The New Religious Intolerance* (2012) are particularly useful in this discussion: thinking critically and employing imagination in the development of empathy. We combine the ideas of these two authors in describing the qualities we need to cultivate in order to build bridges between different faith communities and promote the common good.

Chapter six moves the discussion specifically to college campuses for an exploration of what reflective commitment can look like and how we can cultivate this mature approach to faith within the context of higher education—particularly Christian higher education. The qualities we need in order to constructively engage a religiously diverse world must be considered together, since each informs and shapes the other, helping to maintain a balance of commitment and humble openness to religious others. This balance of reflective commitment and receptive humility is one of the hallmarks of the mature faith we seek to develop.

Some claim that religious exclusivists (those who believe that their religion is the only way to God) can't participate genuinely in interfaith engagement activities. This doesn't have to be the case, though. Exclusivist beliefs can be held with humility and an awareness of one's own fallibility; they can be expressed cautiously, and religious exclusivists can still believe that they have much to learn from their religious neighbors. Christian colleges and Christian student organizations can be communities of strong Christian commitment while at the same time maintaining a thoughtful, open, loving, and humble stance toward religious neighbors.

While the premise of this book is that we have both a civic and theological imperative to move beyond our own religious bubbles, our bubble spaces can be healthy environments for practicing the skills and traits we need for constructive interfaith engagement. Our college classrooms and student organizations can become communities of reflective Christian commitment while at the same time maintaining receptive humility toward religious neighbors. If a classroom or club is to help foster such qualities, we need to provide a balance of support and challenge. We can do this by building trust, practicing hospitality, and lowering perceived risks.

Chapter seven builds on the idea of cultivating healthy bubble spaces by providing several practical ideas that can be used to help develop the transferable skills needed for constructive interfaith engagement. These suggestions include: learning to see from different perspectives by utilizing Peter Elbow's believing and doubting games, making regular space for "community day" conversations that offer an opportunity to ask questions in an atmosphere that shifts the emphasis from debate to dialogue, learning to listen charitably to different voices with a project that involves both research and reflection, and cultivating our imaginations through the use of case studies, role-plays, intrafaith dialogue, and spiritual autobiographies and films.

We can't really show love to our religious neighbors, however, if we never leave the safety and relative homogeneity of our own religious bubbles. Chapter eight explores the idea that, while much learning can and does take place inside the classroom, off-campus learning opportunities are essential for learning to constructively engage a religiously diverse world. First, getting off campus allows us to get to know and interact with people who are genuinely committed to a different religion. This provides a chance, say Douglas and Rhonda Jacobsen, to get to know a religion "as it is actually lived . . . trying to understand how that religion 'works' for the people involved in it."[13] Getting off campus also shifts the power base. We experience what it's like to be the "other" in someone else's religious home. This cultivates a lived empathy that goes beyond what can be developed through in-class activities such as discussing books and watching films. Toward that end we suggest several activities and organizations that can help in planning off-campus learning and service opportunities.

There's a quote from Martin Buber that regularly seems to work its way into our publications, workshops, and conference presentations: "Certainly what one believes is important, but still more important is *how* one believes it."[14] Throughout this book we illustrate Buber's important observation by sharing some personal stories of students, faculty, and staff committed to the work of crossing faith lines. We hope they inspire you, as they inspire us, with pictures of the good that can be accomplished when we leave the security of our bubbles for the better world that can be achieved by building bridges.

The authors of these narratives come from different religious and cultural backgrounds, different college experiences, and different stages of life. Yet together their stories paint a broad picture of what we can accomplish together when we allow love of neighbor to be a stronger motive than fear of difference. Tanden, Amber, and Janna offer personal reflections on why interfaith engagement is an important aspect of their Christian faith. Greg and Rachael, two IFYC alumni who continue to be involved in interfaith work in different ways, share how they live out their Christian faith commitments through getting to know and serving those from other religious and nonreligious backgrounds. Anna and Amy, a former Bethel student and a current Bethel professor, describe how we stand to gain a better sense of ourselves and the world around us when we engage religious diversity. And we close with the stories of April and Ola, two unlikely partners from different religious backgrounds who ended up transforming relationships between Christians and Muslims on their college campus.

For now, here is a story from our own work moving from bubble to bridge. On a cold November afternoon a group of faculty and students piled into vans to drive fifteen minutes south of our suburban campus to an urban mosque attended primarily by Somali Muslims. Although only a few miles away from each other, the two locations seemed worlds apart in terms of class, culture, and religion. Most of our students had never visited a mosque before, nor had they had much opportunity to interact with Somalis or with Muslims. At the entrance to the mosque we split into groups of male and female, removed our shoes, donned headscarves, and embarked on a new experience.

Two hours later we left, having experienced many things. We had toured the mosque and learned about Islamic religious practices as well as the community services that took place there each day. During a time of tea and cookies, students were able to converse informally with each other about many topics, including the experience of being Muslim in the United States, gender roles and relationships, and views of prayer and religious practice. And through a time of intense discussion about similarities and differences between Islam and Christianity, our students saw the sincere devotion and commitment held by people of another faith tradition, the important role that dialogue plays in overcoming misperceptions and stereotypes, and the need for interfaith dialogue and service as we seek to cultivate healthy civic partnerships in the twenty-first century.

Here are some reflections from two of our students about this event. One said:

> Sitting back and always surrounding people with similar views as you will never challenge you. Questioning your faith is not a bad thing. I had never been put in a situation where I was forced to truly look at my faith and say, "You know what, this doesn't make complete logical sense. . . . So why do I believe this?" The trip to the mosque showed me that some aspects of faith will never be able to be scientifically or intelligently proven; it's unfathomable. But part of the awe of God is the fact that although we will never have some answers, he is still willing to reveal himself to us and guide us in our confusion.

Another student said:

> People are so much more than the labels I paint them with. Muslims, Christians, Hindus, Jews—they all have hopes, fears, and dreams, just as I do. People are people. They need to be loved by me, and I need to be loved by them no matter what color their skin is, what culture they have grown up in, or what ideas they hold as true.

1

Why Interfaith Engagement?

A Civic Imperative

"Dialogue or die," says Diana Eck.[1] This might sound like hyperbole, but Eck is hardly alone in making such strong statements. As Warren Nord puts it, "Religious diversity is a massive fact of modernity. This being the case it seems even more obvious now than a decade or two ago that we must learn to live with our deepest differences—which are often religious."[2] Drawing from numerous sources of data, Nord notes that "the majority of people in the world . . . make sense of their lives and the world to some considerable extent in religious categories."[3] Unfortunately, this "resurgence of religion on the world scene" has frequently contributed to horrible violence.[4]

Because much of this violence is occurring at present between Christians and Muslims, Brian McLaren describes more peaceable Muslim-Christian relations as "an urgent matter of planetary survival."[5] It's urgent, he says, because together these two religions account for over half of the world's population, with this proportion expected to climb to two-thirds by the end of this century. Together these groups possess most of the world's wealth and weapons, including nuclear weapons. "Dialogue or die" may not be an exaggeration after all.

Religious conflict stems in part from "the global movements of peoples as economic migrants and political refugees and the global movements of business and technology."[6] Such movements, Eck says, have created increasingly diverse and complex societies in which people are "wrestling with new levels of religious diversity and cultural encounter."[7] In these cultural encounters, "people with radically different backgrounds and values are bound together, yet at the same time may feel endangered by one another."[8] The diversity and cultural encounter in today's emerging global society is part of a "paradigm shift that is reshaping us at every level as a new and far more integrated world."[9] While this shift is exciting in many ways, opening up possibilities for mutual enrichment and a more robust and inclusive civil society, at the same time it's confusing and disconcerting as each of us wonders what changes lie ahead. Even as we seek to be open to learning from others, we wonder how we can remain true to who we are and what we believe.

Religious diversity doesn't have to lead to fear, confusion, or violence, however. Throughout history, strong religious partnerships have been formed across faith lines to promote the common good and bring about social change. One notable example of such a partnership can be seen in the civil rights movement of the 1960s, in which Americans from a wide range of religious traditions (particularly Catholics, Protestants, and Jews) joined together, their efforts inspired and informed by a Hindu (Gandhi). To pursue peace in our century, we have to be willing to build bridges with other religious communities. In this chapter we'll explore the reality of religious diversity around the world and in the United States, articulate the need for civic pluralism, and identify the important role that higher education should play in promoting interfaith engagement as a path forward.

AMERICA: DEVOUT AND DIVERSE

America is unique in terms of its religious diversity and its religious devotion. In their massive study on religion in the United States, Robert Putnam and David Campbell explore the tensions and opportunities that arise from the role religion plays in the lives of Americans. While the number of nonbelievers in the United States has risen over the last few decades, we still have the highest rate of religiosity among industrialized democratic nations.[10] And while the vast majority of Americans identify with a Christian religious tradition, we're a nation of increasing religious diversity. Putnam and Campbell's research has identified that most Americans don't come from religiously homogenous families and neighborhoods. They note that "Americans continue to be unusually devout . . . but the once stark sociological boundaries among our religions have steadily faded over the last century."[11]

Why does religious diversity pose challenges to American society in the twenty-first century? To examine this question, we must first consider how various religious groups perceive each other. According to Putnam and Campbell's research, Jews, Catholics, and mainline Protestants are perceived most favorably, while Mormons, Buddhists, and Muslims receive the most negative response. Societal perceptions of evangelical Protestants and people who aren't religious fall in the middle.[12] So although Americans are devout and diverse, we don't always view the world outside our religious bubbles constructively. We don't treat all religious traditions with equal respect, and we don't appear to be as willing to build bridges with some groups as we are with others.

Of particular concern for those of us who consider ourselves to be devout is the way in which religiosity can actually hamper constructive navigation of religious diversity. While, according to Putnam and Campbell's research, 84 percent of Americans agree with the statement "Religious diversity has been good for America," that number decreases as the religiosity of the person interviewed increases.[13] The groups least likely to favor religious diversity are the group that Putnam and Campbell refer to as "true believers," who make up roughly 10 percent of the American population. "True believers" are those persons who claim to be absolutely certain of God's existence. They're twice as likely as other Americans to attend a weekly religious service, to hold conservative positions on moral issues, and to believe that their religion is the "only one true religion."[14] Given that many of the people who fall into the category of "true believer" are those likely to attend evangelical Christian colleges or universities or to participate in Christian organizations on campus, the question of how to involve this population in interfaith engagement activities is a question we simply must answer.

To avert the kind of religious violence occurring elsewhere, says Eboo Patel, "we have to take religious diversity seriously, and engage interreligious engagement in a very intentional way."[15] The religious freedom in the United States coupled with a longstanding tradition of allowing religiously motivated perspectives to be part of our civic deliberations presents particular opportunities for interfaith dialogue and cooperation. Patel describes the situation this way: The United States is "the most religiously devout country in the West and the most religiously diverse nation in the world in an era of global religious conflict." This combination, he argues, "puts us at the crossroads of the most profound crisis currently facing humanity."[16]

> **We have to take religious diversity seriously, and engage interreligious engagement in a very intentional way.**
>
> **EBOO PATEL**

NEW NEIGHBORS, NEW CHALLENGES

Increasing religious diversity around the globe too often leads to discrimination, hostility, and violence. A 2015 Pew Research Study, for example, found that "roughly a quarter of the world's countries are still grappling with high levels of religious hostilities within their borders."[17] The majority of these hostilities are directed toward Christians and Muslims: Christians experienced harassment in 102 of 198 countries studied, and Muslims experienced harassment in 99 countries.[18] In addition, there's been a "marked increase" in hostilities directed at Jews around the world. The Pew study found that Jews experienced prejudice and harassment in 77 of the 198 countries studied.[19]

While Americans haven't yet experienced the level of religious violence that has erupted in various hot spots around the world, our country isn't immune to the factors that give rise to religious violence. Some find our unprecedented religious diversity threatening. Confusion and uncertainty can lead to violence when coupled with what *New York Times* columnist Thomas Friedman describes as "religious totalitarianism . . . a view of the world that my faith must reign supreme and can be affirmed and held passionately only if all others are abnegated."[20] Those with this perspective at times use terror as their tool. At other times they foment religious prejudice and fear, "causing friction and fragmentation to obstruct commonsense efforts toward harmony and peace."[21] In situations where people already feel vulnerable, where they don't know or trust their neighbors, where the pace of change feels just too threatening, the voices of religious totalitarianism exert dangerous influence.

The situation is exacerbated by media coverage. Stories of unspeakable acts of violence and cruelty attract attention. Strident voices of hatred and dissension drown out the quieter voices of those seeking mutual understanding and peace. This further promotes distrust and reinforces stereotypes about religious others. This has particularly been a problem in parts of the world where hatred and violence have been going on for years. In Israel-Palestine, for example, continued emphasis on the negative aspects of religion has become a self-fulfilling prophecy.[22] This reinforces the view that the differences between Jews and Muslims are intractable, while also emphasizing the role religion can play in fostering conflict and in justifying violence, rather than showing how religion can promote cooperation and peace. Similarly, American media coverage of violence around the world (or of the 9/11 attacks in 2001) hinders meaningful interfaith engagement.

While the United States has yet to see religiously motivated violence on the scale that's been evident in other parts of the world, religious prejudice exists here as well. A religion and diversity study conducted over a three-year period by sociologist Robert Wuthnow provides evidence of such prejudice among respondents who said that they feared religious diversity might be "undermining long-held American values."[23] Large numbers of respondents were even willing to take their fear of religious diversity so far as to "curb the basic rights of non-Western religious groups in the United States" through measures such as making it illegal for Muslim groups to meet.[24] These survey results—as well as much that's been said in recent election seasons—demonstrate how often we fail to be a welcoming and diversity-friendly society.[25]

The election of Keith Ellison to Congress in 2008 provides a vivid example of religious prejudice in the United States. Simply by self-identifying as a Muslim, Ellison received criticism from those who feared that his faith would influence his politics. In particular, controversy raged over his decision to put his hand on the Qur'an (rather than a Bible) while taking the oath of office.[26] Christians running for public office in this country rarely find themselves under such scrutiny.

According to Martha Nussbaum, "In the United States as in Europe, by far the largest number of troubling incidents concern Islam."[27] Muslim women often face discrimination in hiring when they wear the hijab, plans to build mosques or Islamic community centers regularly face strong opposition, and much fear is voiced over the possibility of using shari'a law to settle disputes in America. And Muslims aren't the only religious groups facing religious prejudice in the United States. Nussbaum notes, for example, incidents of Sikhs facing tough scrutiny at TSA checkpoints and an attempt to disrupt the first Hindu prayer offered in the US Senate by protestors claiming to be "Christians and Patriots."[28]

It's clear that we have much work to do to find civic harmony amidst growing religious diversity. In his 2009 inaugural address, President Barack Obama spoke of our "patchwork heritage" as a "strength, not a weakness." The diverse quilt he described wasn't merely one of racial and ethnic diversity but also one of religious diversity, for "we are a nation of Christians and Muslims, Jews and Hindus, and non-believers."[29] In order for diversity to be a strength, however, we must actually choose to build meaningful and constructive relationships with those who believe differently, no matter how scary that proposition may seem.

> **We must actually choose to build meaningful and constructive relationships with those who believe differently.**

THE NEED FOR CIVIC PLURALISM

For several decades the debate surrounding the role of religion in American society has focused on the divide between Christianity and secularism. As the battle lines have been drawn, theorists such as Robert Audi, John Rawls, and Richard Rorty have taken a prominent stance on one side, arguing for the public sphere to be a secular space. Although they differ on whether or not religion should be absolutely excluded from public debate, this camp of philosophers clearly advocates a secular public sphere for contemporary liberal democracies. On the other side, key thinkers such as

Philip Quinn, Jeffrey Stout, and Nicholas Wolterstorff have argued for the legitimacy of religious reasoning in the public sphere.

Two facets of this debate limit the promotion of civic harmony. First, this debate is usually posed between secularism and religion in general, yet it often focuses specifically on tensions between secularism and Christianity. This isn't an accurate picture of our religiously diverse society today, but there hasn't been much work done on either side to acknowledge or explore how America's increasing religious diversity impacts the debate. And focusing the debate on ardent secularism and devout Christianity actually creates a false impression of religious polarization. The reality, according to Putnam and Campbell, is that "most Americans welcome the influence of religion . . . while only a small and highly secularized segment of the population is decidedly unwelcoming. When it comes to the question of religion's role in society America's house may be divided, but not in two equal parts."[30]

Second, the discussion of religion's role in public life often concentrates on the legitimacy of using religious reasons in support of one's position. It's often assumed that the political agent already has her mind made up and simply must choose how to articulate her view publicly. We're interested, however, in promoting the sort of ongoing dialogue that builds mutual understanding and collaborative partnerships that may or may not be rooted in common beliefs and values.

Recognizing that "many religious people aim to shape public life according to their own vision of the good life," some seek to suppress religious voices in the public square, believing that such action will keep religious people from imposing their views on civic life.[31] But this isn't the solution. Religion is important to so many people that it simply can't be excluded from public deliberations about our life together. And because "religious belief is often central to people's lives," says Gustav Niebuhr, "it seems a simple proposition to state that ignorance of religious differences can be perilous."[32] We need to be willing to learn more about our religious neighbors, to build relationships with them, and, ultimately, to seek to "create a new, broader sense of 'we.'"[33]

To accomplish this, we need more than "mere coexistence" among diverse neighbors, says Patel—but neither should we push for a false consensus.[34] Instead we seek to develop a pluralistic society, a society characterized by three things: "respect for people's religious (and other) identities, positive relationships between people of different religious backgrounds, and common action for the common good."[35] And these three characteristics of a pluralistic society are interrelated: A willingness to respect another person's beliefs and spiritual identity can help to nurture a relationship; as relationships grow, respect increases; and respect and relationships help to equip people of diverse beliefs and backgrounds to join together in building a more just and peaceful society. As Rabbi Heschel reminds us, "In spite of fundamental disagreements [between religions] there is a convergence of some of our commitments, of some of our views, tasks we have in common, evils we must fight together, goals we share, a predicament afflicting us all."[36] Interfaith cooperation is important in part because "religions command resources that can be deployed more effectively for common purposes."[37] In addition, such cooperation helps to strengthen social bonds as we get to know our religious neighbors. So we must seek to focus in particular on our shared values rather than on what divides us.

> **While diversity is an inescapable fact of modern life, pluralism is "an achievement" that takes "deliberate and positive engagement of diversity . . . building strong bonds between people from different backgrounds."**
> EBOO PATEL

DISTINGUISHING PLURALISMS: CIVIC VS. THEOLOGICAL

But religions aren't all the same. Some beliefs and teachings are ultimately irreconcilable, and ignoring this fact can be deeply problematic. How can this be resolved? Diana Eck wisely points out that "our theological questions are not quite the same as our civic questions."[38] Theological questions might center around topics such as the path to salvation or the divinity of Christ, for example, and will certainly elicit significant disagreement between people of different faiths. We would argue that, while there is a time and a place to consider such important questions, they should be set aside when exploring civic issues such as "how people of various traditions of faith will relate to each other as co-citizens of a common nation."[39] Patel offers helpful advice along these lines: If we hope to work together for the common good, we need to be willing to "set a safe space where participants acknowledge that we might have different ideas of heaven and how to get there, but that on earth we can work together, and to do so we must respect each other's religious traditions."[40]

Miroslav Volf makes a similar point in his book *Allah: A Christian Response.* In discussing the relationships between Christians and Muslims, Volf focuses on "God and this world, not . . . God and the world to come."[41] He also makes a distinction between what he calls "socially relevant knowledge of God" and "saving knowledge of God."[42] Even though Muslims and Christians are divided when it comes to the latter, they have much in common regarding the former and thus can be "allies in promoting a vision of human flourishing centered on love of God and love of neighbor."[43]

As we seek to do good in the world, to mobilize religious communities to act together to combat poverty and injustice, to build peace together, we do well to remember Jesus' words in Mark 9:40—that "anyone who is not against us is for us." Looking through this lens, we can focus on the similarities between Christians and our religious neighbors rather than on what divides us. We can thus argue that anyone fighting injustice and seeking to protect the vulnerable is "doing Christ's work—even if they don't do it in Christ's name—and Christians can and should work alongside them."[44] If we're willing to set aside theological issues for a time, says Volf, we make it possible to partner with our neighbors, "while living peacefully and constructively together under the same political roof."[45]

> **We don't have to come to a consensus on every theological detail before we can agree to embrace a shared vision of love and justice that crosses religious boundaries.**
> MIROSLAV VOLF

Such a perspective is emphasized in "An Evangelical Manifesto," a statement of evangelical identity that was drafted and published by a group of evangelical leaders in 2008. The authors see this statement as "an example of how different faith communities may address each other in public life, without any compromise of their own faith but with a clear commitment to the common good of the societies in which we all live together."[46] In terms of the manifesto's perspective on religion and public life, the authors state that:

> Our commitment is to a *civil public square—a vision of public life in which citizens of all faiths are free to enter and engage the public square on the basis of their faith, but within a framework of what is agreed to be just and free for other faiths too.* Thus every right we assert for ourselves is at once a right we defend for others.[47]

Fear or Trust?

Returning to Eck's proposition of "dialogue or die," we must understand that the possibility of civic harmony lies in our own hands. One way of framing the difference between these two options is to consider that we have a choice between remaining fragmented in various religious bubbles, allowing the distance between us to foster fear and even hatred, or we can seek to build bridges of trust and partnership between our various communities.

The path of fear is deeply problematic, because it's often both irrational and narcissistic. As Nussbaum explains, fear usually begins with a real anxiety-producing problem, such as economic insecurity or rapid social change. It can become irrational, though, because "fear is easily displaced onto something that may have little to do with the underlying problem but that serves as a handy surrogate for it, often because the new target is already disliked."[48] (It's well known, for example, that Jews became the scapegoat for the economic depression of Germany in the 1920s and 1930s.) Displaced fear is further fueled by the idea that the enemy is hiding, waiting for the opportunity to harm and destroy. Thus displaced fear actually begins to seem like a realistic threat that must be addressed. For example, a small number of Americans believe that Muslims are planning to destroy the United States and create an Islamic state in its absence. Not only do these types of fear lack a credible basis, they also promote an unhealthy narcissism that eclipses our ability to see the humanity of others. Fear focuses primarily on the protection of oneself. It is a "'dimming preoccupation': an intense focus on the self that casts others into darkness. However valuable and indeed essential it is in a genuinely dangerous world, it is itself one of life's great dangers."[49]

What's the antidote to fear? Scripture says that it's love (see, for example, 1 Jn 4:18). In a civic context this means building relationships with others and looking out for their interests as well as our own. When we build meaningful relationships with others, we can no longer hold ignorant, displaced, or false beliefs about them. Instead we build bridges between ourselves and others when we acknowledge our common humanity and share concern for the common good.

Building strong social bonds between people from different social groups, what Robert Putnam calls "bridging capital,"[50] is particularly important in societies of increasing ethnic and social heterogeneity such as our own. Increasing diversity, says Putnam, is "not only inevitable but . . . also desirable," at least over the long run.[51] Numerous sources provide evidence of societal benefits that stem from immigration and diversity.[52] In the short run, however, the picture isn't so positive. A large-scale survey that Putnam and his colleagues conducted revealed that "in more diverse communities, people trust their neighbors less."[53] This occurs, Putnam says, because diversity "seems to trigger . . . social isolation," fostering a kind of "hunker down" mentality.[54] With this mentality in operation, "inhabitants of diverse communities tend to withdraw from collective life," thus experiencing fewer opportunities to get to know their neighbors and to build bonds of social relationship.[55] In fact, residents in such communities often withdraw from civic life so much that they not only fail to build bonds with those outside of their group (with "them"); they fail to build bonds with those inside of their group (with "us"). This is why Putnam and Campbell note that "the United States would appear to be a tinderbox for a religious conflagration."[56]

How can we avert such disaster? We must understand that fear begets fear and trust begets trust. Putnam observes that people who trust others are more likely to participate in their community, and this community engagement in turn reinforces their willingness to trust others and to become trustworthy themselves. "Conversely, the civically disengaged believe themselves to be surrounded by miscreants and feel less constrained to be honest themselves."[57] We must learn to build better relationships with those in our bubbles as well as build bridges with other communities.

Scholars studying social dynamics in volatile parts of the world suggest some ways that bridge-building can help prevent religious violence. In India and Nigeria, two countries where ethnic and religious diversity often erupt horribly, some communities remain peaceful despite "enduring patterns of violence" experienced just miles down the road.[58] The peaceful communities have this in common, observes political scientist Ashutosh Varshney: they've developed "networks of engagement" that cut across various social groups.[59] These networks may seem insignificant at first—a member of one social group shops at a store owned by a member of a different social group; a child from one social group plays with a child from a different group and the parents thus have some contact with each other. Over time, however, such small steps allow people in diverse communities to get to know each other, helping them avoid the "ignorance of the religious other [that] breeds contempt and justifies unfounded negative myths of the other's religious practices and beliefs."[60]

Thus three mutually reinforcing dynamics interact. First, community residents get to know each other as people. Even if this knowledge doesn't lead to close, intimate relationships, it still helps to personalize one's neighbors. Second, social interactions help to develop social capital. In Putnam's discussion of social capital, he differentiates between what he calls "bonding" capital—that which solidifies relationships with those who are most like us—and "bridging" capital—that which helps to build connections across social divides.[61] Both bonding and bridging capital are essential in strengthening the social fabric of a community.

As community residents get to know each other and as social capital (especially bridging capital) begins to develop, a third important dynamic occurs: people learn about the beliefs and practices of their religious neighbors. Such knowledge is particularly crucial when "false claims against each other" are made by members of one religion or another.[62] In violent communities, these false claims multiply because counterclaims aren't made and people lack adequate knowledge to evaluate for themselves. But in peaceful communities, folks interact regularly across religious lines, helping to dispel false claims and combat religious prejudice and hatred. They're able to develop a "healthy knowledge of the different religious claims and practices of their neighbors."[63]

EDUCATING TOWARD CIVIC PLURALISM

If we hope to support a civil public square and foster a healthy, robust society in which people of diverse beliefs can join together as true neighbors, then education must prepare students for such civic participation. Contributors to the Wingspread Declaration on Religion and Public Life concur. In July 2005, scholars from public and private colleges and universities—representing diverse disciplines, geographic regions, and faith perspectives—gathered to discuss "the growing awareness of and concern over the intersection between religion and public life and to define the role that higher education must play in response to those concerns."[64] The statement that resulted from this gathering asserts that we must support deliberative democracy by committing to "principles of inclusiveness and respect as foundations for dissent, dialogue, and action. . . . It is the academy's responsibility to model a more positive, productive, and educationally sound form of engagement."[65]

Warren Nord agrees. The contentiousness we too often encounter in America's public square must be counteracted by educators who "nurture the virtue of civility" in which we "respect the rights of others" as well as seek to understand one another's views.[66]

Colleges and universities, and the student organizations on their campuses, are well-positioned to foster the type of social change needed to cultivate a healthy civic pluralism. As Patel notes, students need help developing a "vocabulary that helps them stay grounded in their own tradition and relate positively to those from other traditions."[67] Increasing our interfaith literacy helps to meet this need in three ways. It builds "appreciative knowledge of other traditions," it helps us "identify values that all religious share," and it nurtures an "understanding of the history of interfaith cooperation in our nation and our world."[68] By embracing interfaith literacy as a goal, we have the opportunity to gain knowledge and develop relationships that will "challenge the stereotypes" of religious others and work to "advance an alternative narrative."[69]

Faculty, staff, and students at predominantly Christian institutions or in predominantly Christian organizations share this responsibility and, at the same time, face unique challenges, particularly if there's little religious diversity on campus. We encourage our students to see possible connections between their beliefs and their academic learning and social experiences—very important parts of our institutional missions—but students on many of our campuses have limited opportunities to interact directly with persons who practice a religious or spiritual tradition different from their own.

This is a problem. Students need to become more aware of the world into which they'll graduate, in which they'll live and work with people whose beliefs differ.[70] It's also a problem because without such direct knowledge of religious difference, students may not learn how to interact effectively in religiously diverse contexts. To interact effectively in such contexts, we need to be able to distinguish between what Diana Eck calls a "civic" and a "theological" voice.[71] When speaking in a civic voice, we need to learn to employ what Eck calls "bridging speech," which is "not spoken in the particular dialect of a single religious tradition."[72] Bridging speech is best developed through facilitated dialogue and the relationships that can develop through conversation and shared acts of service.

Interfaith dialogue linked with acts of service not only helps develop bridging speech. It also helps build the kind of bridging capital that Putnam argues is so essential in a diverse society, which in turn will "strengthen America's civic fabric and . . . show the world that conflict between faiths is so far from inevitable."[73] Interfaith engagement thus has civic value because it demonstrates our belief in and commitment to the formation of a society that seeks to respect differences while also building on our commonalities—a mindset that seeks to combat "a contested realm of us-versus-them."[74]

> **Interfaith engagement thus has civic value because it demonstrates our belief in and commitment to the formation of a society that seeks to respect differences while also building on our commonalities.**

CONCLUSION

For many Christians, the situation is complicated. We want to be good citizens and helpful neighbors, finding ways to build bridges with others by focusing on our commonalities. At the same time, however, we fear what might be lost in the process—such as Christianity's unique claims and our understanding of our own identities as believers. Will we be forced into an untenable compromise if we keep seeking to speak in a civic voice? Should we grieve the loss of Christianity's prevalence and influence in American society? What does it mean to be a faithful follower of Christ today? How should we talk about our Christian identity in a religiously diverse world?

"We need a language that maintains our own distinctiveness and truth claims while respecting the goodness in others and, above all, affirming the holiness of the relationships," one Christian youth ministry leader observes.[75] This is particularly challenging because "the most prevalent Christian language in the public square is the language of domination."[76] As Christians, we have the opportunity to change our voice from one of domination to one of love. In the next chapter, we'll explore the unique responsibility we have to promote the common good by following the two most important commandments—loving God and loving others.

Talk About It

- Discuss the difference between civic pluralism and theological pluralism. How do Christian belief and practice support the idea of civic pluralism?

- How is religion being covered in current media stories? Does the coverage seem to promote a climate of fear or trust?

- In what ways can interfaith dialogue be valuable for civic life?

Give It a Try

Research a recent issue of religious tension in your own local community or at the national level. Identify the ways in which a lack of interfaith engagement is hindering progress on this issue. Imagine what it would look like to build interfaith bridges in this context.

THE WORLD IS A REALLY BIG PLACE

Tanden Brekke, assistant director of community engagement and service learning, Bethel University

In 2012 as part of a budding relationship, the Minnesota Da'wah Institute invited representatives from Bethel University to celebrate an iftar dinner. Growing up in a Christian context, I had never celebrated an iftar dinner, but I knew that this was a special occasion and I felt honored by the invitation. At this point in my life I was thirty-six, had a master's degree in theology, and had been a Christian pastor for twelve years, yet I had had few authentic interfaith interactions. I knew that I wanted my children to experience religious differences much earlier in life, so I invited my son Micah, who was ten, to join me. I gave him a brief lesson about Ramadan and the role that the iftar dinner plays in the fast, and then we headed out to be welcomed into an experience that was outside of our norm.

We joined several other students, staff, and faculty from Bethel University at the Da'wah Institute for an evening that was filled with prayer, food, conversations, and gracious hospitality. It was a wonderful time for Christians to engage with our Muslim sisters and brothers in a way that broke down many of the stereotypes that Christians have of Muslims. As we got into the car to drive home, my thoughts were racing from the experience. Through the crowd of thoughts in my mind, I got the idea to ask Micah the very simple question, "What did you think about that experience?" His answer still brings tears of joy to my eyes every time I reflect on it. He told me, "Dad, the world is a really big place, and I have only experienced a very small part of it."

Dad, the world is a really big place, and I have only experienced a very small part of it.

He went on to tell me that the sounds, images, and tastes that he had experienced that night were very different from what was normative to him. Those differences revealed to him a beautifully diverse world. As we reflected on our experience that night, a hunger grew in both of us to engage with religious diversity. We both talked about our longings to live in this world in such a way as to be open to and seeking out these beautiful experiences. We also talked about the many different forces that push us to stay within our isolated Christian community, and how we need to be intentional to work against those forces if we really want to engage in a religiously diverse world.

That interfaith experience, as well as the work of interfaith solidarity that I have been a part of since that time, is teaching me just how easy it is for Christians in a "Christian nation" to live in a limited world with very little interaction with religious others. This insular world nurtures us to believe in a small, oversimplified version of the actual world. We quickly start to discount the experiences of others and we live in such a way that privileges our experiences as normative. Our curiosity becomes stunted and we become incapable of seeing the beautifully vivid colors of the world. As we step out of our normative experiences and encounter others, these experiences rapture us up in ways that we could never have anticipated. We become sensitive to others' experiences, we hold our own beliefs with more humility, and we become more responsive to the gracious invitations that are extended to us by others.

> **Interfaith solidarity welcomes us into a way of living where we are able to see more images, smell more smells, hear more sounds, and participate in justice in ways that we never could when we only see life through our own religious tradition.**

Interfaith solidarity welcomes us into a way of living where we are able to see more images, smell more smells, hear more sounds, and participate in justice in ways that we never could when we only see life through our own religious tradition. The question that is ever before me is: Will I continue to follow the Spirit of God into this beautifully diverse world?

2

Why Interfaith Engagement?

A Religious Imperative

In a familiar passage in the New Testament, Jesus states that the
entire religious law is reducible to two principles: "Love the LORD
your God with all your heart, all your soul, and all your mind" and
"Love your neighbor as yourself" (Mt 22:37-39). While most Christians easily recognize these commands as essential, many don't
really unpack their full meaning. There are shining examples of
Christian involvement in social action growing out of such love—
founding hospitals, seeking to abolish slavery, fighting for social
justice throughout the world. But among many American Christians, the track record isn't so great when it comes to our treatment
of religious neighbors.

In the early decades of the twentieth century, for example, conservative Protestants engaged in much fearmongering rhetoric
against Catholic Christians (such as John F. Kennedy) and the
"threat" they posed to America.[1] Today, such rhetoric is no longer
being employed against Catholics, but it does represent the attitude
of many Christians toward Muslims.[2] The experience that Brian
McLaren describes from his own evangelical upbringing provides
an all-too-common example of such an attitude toward Muslims:

"Be nice to them when necessary in order to evangelize them; otherwise, see them as spiritual competitors and potential enemies."[3] This attitude doesn't reflect Christians acting out of love for their religious neighbors! The truth is that when Jesus commands us to love our neighbors, he means love everyone, even those who believe differently from us. In fact many of Jesus' most daring acts of love involved those who weren't "good Jews": the Samaritan woman at the well, Zacchaeus the tax collector, and the woman caught in adultery, to name a few.

In the nineteenth century, Danish philosopher Søren Kierkegaard wrote a lengthy reflection on these commandments to love God and neighbor titled *Works of Love*. In this work Kierkegaard explores important questions regarding who we are to love and what that love should look like. Although he doesn't discuss religious diversity directly, the book does have clear implications for loving our religious neighbors. According to Kierkegaard, love of neighbor isn't the same as the preferential love of friendship. God isn't commanding us simply to love those people who are most like us or with whom we choose to be in relationship. Rather, "The Christian teaching . . . is to love one's neighbor, to love all mankind, all men, even enemies, and not to make exceptions, neither in favoritism nor in aversion."[4]

According to Kierkegaard, love of neighbor is the best way to express Christ's own love for us. Love of neighbor requires that we go beyond knowledge or awareness of the other's existence and actually become a neighbor to that person. It is something that, according to Kierkegaard, we prove through compassionate acts.[5] This is particularly important in the context of persons who believe differently. As Kierkegaard explains, love doesn't mean trying to make someone become like me, "substitut[ing] an imaginary idea of how we think or could wish that this person should be."[6] Instead, Kierkegaard argues that we have a continuous duty to love the other as neighbor, regardless of his or her acts or beliefs, because in the other we can see the "common watermark" of God's love that's been impressed upon each of us.[7] Fulfilling the command to love the neighbor as ourselves in part fulfills the command to love God.[8]

The title of Kierkegaard's book itself, *Works of Love*, reminds us that responding to all of our neighbors in love is a duty, a work we must do. This emphasis reminds us that love of neighbor isn't based on preference or convenience. "Such a love stands and does not fall with the contingency of its subject but stands and falls with the Law of eternity—but then, of course, it never fails."[9] To deepen our understanding of this duty to love our religious neighbor, we turn next to literature from Christian perspectives on hospitality.

In her examination of hospitality among early Christians, Amy Oden identifies four "movements" in the practice of hospitality: welcoming, restoring, dwelling together, and sending forth. The one who seeks to practice hospitality must first be welcoming, says Oden. Welcoming consists of an "offer to serve, whether implicit or explicit."[10] It may entail receiving a visitor or it may be initiated by the host.[11] The second movement of hospitality, restoring, involves seeking to address the guest's most immediate needs.[12] Dwelling together follows. While "dwelling," the host practices what Oden calls a "hospitality of presence," showing a willingness to share even the uninteresting details of the guest's life and inviting the guest to share with the host in turn. The fourth movement of hospitality, sending forth, consists of a "release, letting go of the stranger or guest with whom one has dwelt."[13] This act of letting go is made possible because the preceding acts of hospitality have restored and empowered the guest.

PREPARING TO PRACTICE HOSPITALITY

To demonstrate love and hospitality to our religious neighbors, we must first prepare ourselves to be good hosts. A first step in this

self-preparation is to stop seeing religious others "most fundamen-
tally as enemies . . . and strangers" and to come to see them as
"fellow creatures . . . and neighbors."[14] This shift in perspective helps
us focus on what we have in common rather than focusing on what
divides us. And this sense of connection helps to create an "inner
space" that isn't just an "empty room, waiting passively to be filled
by whoever happens to drop by." Instead, it's more like a "laboratory
in which new modes of welcoming and being welcomed are
created."[15] In such a space many new things become possible, including the "hope—even the presumption—that grace is what one
will meet in the encounter with the stranger."[16]

To be prepared to meet such grace, we need to heed the recurring voices of early Christian writers who remind us to expect
surprises.[17] One such surprise is that "the apparent stranger is . . .
Christ himself. . . . In receiving others, we receive Christ. In rejecting them, we reject Christ."[18] Many Christians are familiar with
such notions of hospitality—including Christ's own words that "I was a stranger and you welcomed me" (Mt 25:35, NRSV). But are we willing to welcome our religious neighbors as we would welcome Christ?

Focus on what we have in common rather than focusing on what divides us.

Can we see the rabbi we meet at the farmer's market as a person
who can bring Christ's word to us? What about the Muslim family
who lives nearby? The "Christ at the door," observes Oden, is "rarely
the Christ we expect or the Christ of our imaginings."[19]

WELCOME AND RESTORATION AS ACTS OF LOVE

Many who write about hospitality address the host's responsibility to
create an environment that's "welcoming, affirming, and safe."[20] In
creating this kind of environment, the host lavishes "loving attention"

on the guest, "grant[ing] space" to the guest's voice.[21] Such attentiveness helps promote inclusion and respect that, in time, can "powerfully reframe social relations and engender welcome," says Oden.[22] While the host recognizes and seeks to meet the needs of her guest—perhaps physical needs for food or shelter, emotional needs to feel welcomed, or other needs—practicing hospitality also means the host will view her guest as a person made in God's image, loved by God, worthy of dignity and respect, with unique thoughts and experiences, from whom the host can learn. Failure to keep this in mind can "lead to our patronizing others and ultimately treating them as no better than objects."[23]

While hospitality involves thoughtfully giving gifts, of equal importance is the host's willingness to receive what the guest has to offer. In fact, the same Greek word (*xenos*) is used in ancient literature for both "guest" and "host," and "many early Christian texts deliberately confuse the roles of host and guest" to such an extent that "it is sometimes hard to tell who is giving and who is receiving."[24] This leads some to argue that we have a "social duty" to receive from our guests rather than simply seeking to give to them. Because, says Anthony Gittins, receiving "empowers . . . the giver," showing the recipient's willingness to place herself "however temporarily—in an inferior position" which makes it possible for the relationship to "move to one of reciprocity and mutuality."[25]

> The host's role is to learn from the guest rather than to attempt to change the guest.
>
> **HARRY MURRAY**

Imagine how welcoming and restorative it can be for religious neighbors to be treated with respect by the Christians they encounter, to have these Christians treat them as if their spiritual lives are genuine and meaningful—and that this is a part of them from which Christians can learn. For example, Christians can learn from their religious neighbors by listening to the insights and experiences gained from various spiritual disciplines and practices common to numerous religions. We can listen to Muslim neighbors speak of their experiences with fasting. We can listen to Jewish neighbors reflect on the practice of saying prayers for the dead in community with others who seek to honor God amid their grief. We can learn from Buddhist neighbors how to cultivate mindfulness.

DWELLING AND SENDING AS ACTS OF LOVE

It's one thing to welcome a guest, even listening for a short time to what that person has to say. But the next stage of hospitality—Oden calls it "dwelling"—can be particularly challenging.[26] We may feel challenged and surprised to "find beauty" in other faiths, even those faiths that we were "raised to think were wrong, even evil."[27] We may, to our chagrin, discover that someone of a different faith lives out the values of our own faith better than we do.[28] When this occurs, we may even experience what's been described as "'holy envy'—the sensation of learning about a tradition, practice, or concept in another's religion that you wish you had in your own faith."[29] Such experiences may challenge us to rethink our understanding of ourselves as people of faith, as well as rethinking the commonalities and differences among religions.

We may know that hospitality includes "making room for the different and new values that the guest might bring."[30] The challenge comes, however, when we begin to experience "tension between being open to our guests and preserving our own values and identity."[31] This is no simple matter. It takes real discernment to determine which values are central to my identity as a Christian and which are peripheral. It also takes discernment to determine when to speak and when to ask questions or listen quietly. In addition, the possibility exists, of course, that my understanding of a theological issue is actually a distortion and that my religious neighbor's understanding is closer to the truth. Thus, what feels challenging or even threatening to me may prove to be exactly what I need to hear. This is one reason why we need to welcome guests: to help "broaden our understanding and grasp of the truth."[32]

In many such situations we must be willing to reexamine our theological notions, to practice what Livingstone Thompson calls a "theology of modesty," which he describes as "a theological discourse that takes place with a keen awareness of the limits of human knowledge of the divine life."[33] A proponent of such modesty was Nikolaus von Zinzendorf, an eighteenth-century pietist who, consistent with the emphases of that Christian movement, placed a particularly strong emphasis on love of neighbor. Thompson notes that Zinzendorf, in his reading of the early chapters of Genesis, sees the fall as a "lust of the mind, a seeking to know where one should be keen to love. God's conversation with Adam was in effect a critique of those who were more concerned with insight and reflection than with love."[34] Perhaps some of our failures to show hospitality to our religious neighbors arise out of an undue emphasis on "insight and reflection" rather than placing the emphasis where it should be—on love.

As we take time to dwell with our religious neighbors, we encounter additional important perspectives. First, we gain an insider's perspective on what it looks like to believe and practice a religion other than our own. To gain such a perspective, we go beyond trying to understand others from our own vantage point, instead listening attentively in order to "understand the religious other in a way that the other can recognize himself or herself in my perception."[35] This kind of listening isn't the sort that Christians usually practice toward their religious neighbors. Often we listen selectively, "looking for flaws in what the other person has to say, mentally preparing for ways to demonstrate the superiority of Christianity over the other person's religion."[36]

At the very least we Christians can love our religious neighbors by listening to them talk about their understanding of God, their sacred scriptures, and their spiritual practices. In so doing we can learn about another religion from a new vantage point, and we get to know our neighbors as people with faith lives they care deeply about—just as we care about ours. This is important to keep in mind because to dismiss the significance of a faith "to which people commit their lives in all sincerity . . . becomes a dismissal of the significance of the adherents themselves."[37] We show love and hospitality to our religious neighbors when we respect their faith lives even when we disagree with them.[38]

As we dwell with our religious neighbors and learn more about their perspective on their own faith, we also learn more about their perspective on our faith. At times this knowledge can help us correct their misperceptions of Christianity, or at least complicate the picture by showing them that not all Christians think or believe or behave alike. At other times we may find ourselves surprised or even challenged by critiques of the ways that Christians have treated those outside the church. We must listen to and heed such critiques if we hope to practice hospitality.[39]

In particular, evangelical Christians need to listen carefully to ways in which mission and evangelistic efforts have been received. Some efforts have certainly been wrongheaded in every way; other efforts may grow out of good intentions but still feel offensive to would-be targets of evangelism. For example, given the often violent history between Christians and Muslims, "many Muslims see Christian mission as war by other means," observes Volf.[40] Even if we ourselves aren't the guilty party, we need to examine ourselves and our Christian traditions honestly, learning from our neighbors about the (unintended) harm that other Christians have done to them—and perhaps the (unintended) harm we ourselves have done. Responding in love to such harm now becomes part of our duty as

Christians. Ensuring that other Christians become aware of what we've learned also becomes a way to show love and demonstrate hospitality by preventing similar harm from continuing to occur.

The challenging conversations made possible by relationships forged through dwelling also help remind us that we aren't the only people seeking to be good hosts to our religious neighbors. We too are potential guests of our religious neighbors who hope to show God's love to us. At the same time we may be surprised and even upset to learn that we ourselves may be the "enemy strangers that others are struggling to welcome."[41] This is why it's so important that we take time to listen, to get to know our religious neighbors, to practice the hospitality of dwelling.

Eventually dwelling (Oden's third "movement" of hospitality) will come to an end, leading to the fourth movement—sending. Just as the first three movements of hospitality entail risk (particularly the "uncomfortable and sometimes painful possibility of being changed by the other"[42]), so too with the act of sending. There is, of course, the risk that the guest won't want to be hosted by us again or that she won't want to reciprocate with her own offer of hospitality. There's also the risk that, even if guests have gratefully received the various gifts offered by the host, these same receivers may reinterpret these gifts in order to fit them into their own religious outlook.[43] But "good givers," says Volf, "respect the integrity of receivers. . . . Granting the right of others to receive what they want and do with it as they see fit is part of the respect that givers afford to recipients."[44] Amid such risk—

> **Good givers respect the integrity of receivers.**
> **MIROSLAV VOLF**

of misunderstanding or rejection or confusion—we must "trust . . . that participation in hospitality is participation in the life of God" and trust that God is in charge of the consequences.[45]

LOVE FIGHTS RELIGIOUS PREJUDICE

Loving our religious neighbors goes beyond our personal interactions with them. Hospitality also implies a responsibility to support religious others at the social and political level, and an important way to provide such support is to fight religious prejudice. Regarding Muslim-Christian relationships in particular, Volf observes that "the best way to fight prejudice is by knowledge—not just knowledge of people's beliefs and practices, but knowledge of their feelings and hopes, their injuries and triumphs."[46] If Volf is right, then Christians have a lot of learning to do, both about other religions in general and about individual religious neighbors. And in order to learn well, "we need to be deliberate in seeking out such encounters and then in counteracting falsehoods and misperceptions expressed by fellow Christians about other faiths."[47]

Of course, this is easier said than done, in part because we're impeded by numerous preconceptions about other religions, and these preconceptions make it difficult for us to see possible commonalities between our faith and that of our religious neighbors. Such preconceptions tend to magnify differences and can contribute to religious prejudice. For example, many Christians view Christianity as a religion of grace, whereas they see religions such as Islam as more "legalistic," centered on human efforts to please a demanding God. Christians who believe Islam to be legalistic tend to view comments from a Muslim about God's greatness or power or holiness as confirmation of their views, not even noticing the many times Muslims speak of God's grace and mercy. Another problematic preconception is evident when Christians see Islam as a religion that promotes violence in the name of God while failing to see the numerous instances, both historical and contemporary, of Christians invoking God to justify horrific acts of violence.[48] This notion of Islam as inherently violent has led to numerous acts of physical and verbal violence against Muslim civilians around the world, making them "the most overtly targeted and besieged minority in the West in the post-9/11 era."[49] We are complicit in such discrimination when we don't prepare ourselves to challenge preconceptions and speak out against harmful misconceptions.

Love Refuses to Bear False Witness

If we allow misinformation and stereotypes about our religious neighbors to persist, we not only fail to show love; we're also guilty of bearing false witness. This is why many argue that the commandment against bearing false witness "is the beginning point of a theological mandate for interfaith engagement."[50] We can't be sure that we're telling the truth about our religious neighbors if we haven't taken time to get to know them, listening to what they have to say. Thus, failure to do so is not only inhospitable, but it makes us guilty of lying and of failing to honor others. Volf describes the situation this way: "My distorted image of you dishonors you; I do you injustice by clinging to it. Prejudice is injustice. . . . Prejudice and demonization are forms of falsehood, and falsehood in assessing others is always a form of injustice."[51]

> The commandment against bearing false witness "is the beginning point of a theological mandate for interfaith engagement."
> DOUGLAS PRATT

Sometimes falsehood creeps in when Christians seek to persuade their religious neighbors to turn from their own faith and instead consider Christianity. Seeking to convince others that belief in Christ is superior to other faiths, we may at times bear false witness by misrepresenting faiths other than our own.[52] Recognizing the temptations in this regard, representatives from several international Christian organizations—World Council of Churches, Pontifical Council for Interreligious Dialogue, and World Evangelical Alliance—produced and endorsed a document in 2011 that includes recommendations for Christian witness in a multireligious world. This document includes numerous imperatives about the way we ought to treat our religious neighbors, including the following:

- Avoid condescension and disparagement.

- Speak sincerely and respectfully.

- Listen in order to learn about and understand others' beliefs and practices. Acknowledge and appreciate what is true and good in them.

- Don't bear false witness concerning other religions.

- Avoid misrepresenting the beliefs and practices of people of different religions.[53]

LOVE IS GUIDED BY THE GOLDEN RULE

Although there's much to be learned by listening to our religious neighbors, at times Christians also wish to speak of their own faith in hopes that others may be attracted to Christ. Love certainly might (and often does) motivate us, but Volf argues that many of our religious neighbors don't see mission work and various evangelistic efforts as reflections of love. There may be numerous reasons for this, of course, some of which (such as failing to demonstrate hospitality by welcoming and listening and learning, or by failing to combat religious misinformation and prejudice) we've already discussed. In addition to these reasons, Volf identifies what he describes as a failure to be guided by the golden rule when we speak of Christ to our religious neighbors.

The golden rule of witnessing, says Volf, tells us to "witness to others in the way you think others should witness to you."[54] It seems obvious, then, that we would avoid tactics such as those used by street corner preachers who point fingers at passersby, shouting insults and accusations. It also seems obvious that we'd oppose various scare tactics that some Christian youth groups use in order to impress teenagers with the seriousness of sin and the horrors of hell. Perhaps less obvious, though, is our tendency to "compare the best practices of one's own faith with the worst practices of the other faith," says Volf.[55] This, too, demonstrates a violation of the golden rule, a failure to love our religious neighbor as we love ourselves.

The golden rule of witnessing also tells us to "witness to others only if you are prepared to let them witness to you," says Volf.[56] Many of our religious neighbors take their spiritual lives and religious practices seriously, just as Christians do. And many of these same neighbors want to share the peace and joy they've gained from their own faith, just as Christians do. We might, then, show love and hospitality to our religious neighbors by considering what Brian McLaren says about missions: "Sharing is . . . always about receiving as well as giving. In generosity, we freely share our treasures with people of other faiths. . . . And in the same spirit, we gratefully receive the treasures generously offered to us."[57]

LOVE WORKS WITH OTHERS FOR THE COMMON GOOD

When we join with our religious neighbors in working for the common good, we demonstrate love—for the recipients of our efforts as well as for the neighbors with whom we engage in such efforts. The needs in our world are great, requiring much energy and creative thinking and cooperation. People of faith from a wide array of backgrounds and religions are natural workers in these efforts, regardless of our theological differences. Rowan Williams, Anglican bishop and theologian, addresses Christians and Muslims in this regard, noting that "our voice in the conversation of society will be the stronger for being a joint one." In following God's command to love, he continues, "we need to find ways of being far more effective in influencing our societies to follow the way of God in promoting that which leads to human flourishing."[58] Williams, while acknowledging that the differences between Christians and Muslims are "real and serious," observes that a "focus on love of God and neighbor . . . could be the center of a shared sense of calling and shared responsibility" between us.[59]

It's important to recognize the civic imperative and the religious imperative to love our religious neighbors. Understanding these imperatives isn't enough to motivate interfaith engagement for some, though. As we'll see in chapter three, three primary barriers make it difficult for us to be good religious neighbors: a "conflicted" Christian identity, the social status ambiguity experienced or perceived by many American evangelicals, and fear of our religious neighbors. Two of Christ's parables help provide a picture of what it might look like to act from love rather than fear when interacting with our religious neighbors.

TALK ABOUT IT

- In the past, have you thought of persons from other religious traditions as "neighbors"? Why or why not?

- Describe a time when you were a guest and experienced hospitality. How were you treated? How did this make you feel? Have you ever had the opposite experience?

- Where is religious prejudice happening around you? What would a loving response to that prejudice look like?

GIVE IT A TRY

- Chapter seven contains many practical ideas for implementing the ideas in this book. Use the "Learning to Listen" project described on pages 139-43 as a way to practice welcoming, receiving, and dwelling.

- Reread the recommendations for Christian witness in a multireligious world (see the "Love Does Not Bear False Witness" section earlier in this chapter). Focus on living out one of these recommendations to address in your life over the next few weeks.

I WANT TO KNOW MY NEIGHBORS

Janna B., student and Better Together leader, Bethel University

I believe that interfaith engagement is imperative for me as a follower of Christ. Throughout my grade school, middle school, and high school years, I had several friends with faiths very similar to my own, but I also had a few friends with faiths different from my own. The only message I had received from my church regarding my friends of other faiths or nonfaiths was that I should share my faith with these friends in the hope that they would convert. As a result, I always tried to avoid talking about my Christian faith with these friends, because I did not want to cause tension or feel like if they did not become a Christian, I had failed them as a friend. I also grew up hearing a lot of stereotypes about persons of other faiths or nonfaiths, but I never really took the time or the effort to question those stereotypes.

During the summer after my first year of college, I worked as a nurse's aid in home health care. One of my clients and her husband were Jewish Holocaust survivors, and another client and her husband were Palestinian Muslim refugees. I spent a lot of time with both of these clients and their families. While I was caring for my Jewish client, I listened to her husband share stories of the horrors of the Holocaust. I listened to him reflect on how his faith in God had provided him with comfort during those terrible times and how because of his Jewish faith, he believed in treating all people equally and forgiving those who had wronged him, yet never forgetting what they had done.

While I cared for my Muslim client, I listened to stories of her family back home and her sorrow at her inability to see them. I listened to her reflections on how her faith in Allah gave her the strength to make it through each day and how her practice of waking up very early every morning to pray provided her with a sense of peace amidst her hardships.

Through getting to know my clients, I realized that I could not really care for them without knowing their identities as persons of faith. I also realized that the stereotypes I had heard about persons of other faiths were completely harmful and only succeeded in bringing distance rather than promoting relationships.

So now I am interested in interfaith simply because I want to know people. I strongly believe that a person's faith or nonfaith is a huge component of her or his identity. How can I follow Christ's command to love my neighbor as myself if I fail to know my neighbor's identity as a person of faith? I'm not interested in attempting to figure out if someone's religious or nonreligious beliefs are "true" or not. I'm also not interested in making sure everyone becomes a Christian with an identical faith to mine. I just want to know my neighbors who I believe are all created in the image of God, and I want to build relationships based on our common humanity rather than walls and divisions due to stereotypes.

I just want to know my neighbors who I believe are all created in the image of God, and I want to build relationships based on our common humanity rather than walls and divisions due to stereotypes.

3

Aren't We Better Off in the Bubble?

Remedies from Two Parables

As Christians, we want to learn to contribute productively to society, to partner with others in addressing the needs we encounter, to be good citizens. We also want to be good and loving neighbors. Yet this often proves difficult, particularly when our neighbors' faith commitments differ from our own. It's one thing to check someone's mail when they're on vacation or to chat with a neighbor while out walking the dog. But when a tragedy occurs, does a good Christian neighbor participate in a multifaith prayer service? Does a good Christian neighbor provide a space in her business for Muslim employees to pray? What about helping to support the construction of a nearby mosque?

Examples like these raise questions that help demonstrate some of the complexities for Christians living in a religiously diverse society. Recognizing the loss of Christian dominance in America, we may feel threatened, afraid of what may lie ahead, sad about the loss of the "good old days." Some Christians, in response to this change, may believe that faithful Christ-followers must "fight the good fight" and combat all that isn't clearly and exclusively Christian. Amid change and diversity, it's easy to be led by fear, taking a hostile and combative stance toward people of other faiths. Yet we also recognize and want to fulfill our Christian responsibility to love our neighbors. At such times we may feel stuck, asking ourselves questions: "To accept and love God, must I betray my neighbor of another religion? To accept and love my neighbor, must I betray the God of my religion?"[1]

In this chapter we'll explore three major obstacles to interfaith engagement: a "conflicted" Christian identity, the dynamic of Christian privilege in American society, and the unproductive fear that results from the first two. We don't believe that these obstacles create a hopeless situation when it comes to loving religious neighbors, however. Instead, we follow Patel's advice—that we should each draw on the resources in our faith traditions that "speak to positive relations with the religious other."[2] Two such resources that we'll focus on come from familiar Gospel stories: the parable of the lost son and the parable of the good Samaritan.

CONFLICTED CHRISTIAN IDENTITY

What kind of Christian identity truly honors God and neighbor? Particularly for evangelical Christians living in a multifaith context, it's common to define and describe our identity primarily in terms of how our faith is different from that of non-Christians. We don't want to be judgmental or offensive, but we also want to ensure that we aren't compromising our commitments. We want our faith to remain strong and vibrant and our witness clear. Thus we emphasize ways in which we think Christianity differs from other religions.

Of course it's natural to use words like "we" and "they" when talking about religion and other important identity-defining issues, but this approach to Christian identity is problematic. It's easy to lose sight of the fact that "*we* is not neutral. . . . *They* is a word that pushes away. . . . It draws a boundary, a perimeter, a distinction, a separation, a distance."[3] Gradually, what might have started as a simple effort to clarify distinctions between faith communities leads us to start seeing ourselves and our group as morally and intellectually superior to others. "We" know and are committed to following the truth; "they" are easily thought of as simply "the lost," the "condemned" who are fooling themselves with their empty religious gestures and false beliefs—rather than as neighbors with whom we have much in common and from whom we have something to learn. A focus on religious differences reinforces "us" and "them," leading to a mindset that says our interactions with people of other faiths ought to focus on how our faith is superior. Thus we say things among ourselves like, "Our God is more loving." "Only we truly understand forgiveness." "We're the only ones who are ultimately capable of doing real good in the world."

> *We is not neutral. . . . They is a word that pushes away.*
> MARK LABBERTON

In his recent book *Why Did Jesus, Moses, the Buddha, and Mohammed Cross the Road?*, Brian McLaren uses the term "conflicted religious identity syndrome" to describe the dilemma faced by many evangelical Christians. McLaren says this syndrome emerges during a simultaneous struggle to maintain a strong commitment to one's own faith tradition while seeking to avoid hostility toward people of other faiths. These are both important goals. The problem arises when a person assumes that strong, loyal Christianity is best demonstrated through actively opposing all other faiths.[4] And such Christians often insist that they aren't being hostile but are merely being faithful.[5] So we're left with an internal tension: "How do we remain loyal to what is good and real in our faith without giving tacit support to what is wrong and dangerous? How do we, as

Christians, faithfully affirm the uniqueness and universality of Christ without turning that belief into an insult or a weapon?"[6] These are important questions!

To understand this tension further, McLaren observes that many American Christians today have placed themselves and other Christians along a continuum of "conservative" to "liberal."[7] This continuum is based on the assumption that the "conservative" label describes those with the stronger commitment to Christianity—a commitment best demonstrated by opposition to other religions. Correlatively, the more "liberal" end of the spectrum corresponds with greater tolerance toward other religions, and this tolerance is seen by "conservatives" as corresponding to a weaker commitment to one's own faith identity.[8] But notice what this way of categorizing Christian identity omits: the possibility of a strong faith identity that manifests itself in strong "benevolence, generosity, and hospitality toward others."[9]

Loving our religious neighbors doesn't require abandoning our own faith commitments. Instead, it can flow from an incredibly strong and deep commitment to follow Jesus' teaching that the greatest commandments are to love God and neighbor. In loving our neighbors well, we actually affirm what we believe is good and right about

> **Loving our religious neighbors doesn't require abandoning our own faith commitments.**

our own traditions. What better way to present our faith than to attempt to love others as Christ loves them?

THE COMPLEXITY OF CHRISTIAN PRIVILEGE

Even if we accept that loving our religious neighbors would affirm rather than diminish our Christian identity, we face another challenge when it comes to interfaith engagement: Christian privilege, a complicated reality in American society that can distort Christians' self-perceptions and impede our efforts to form loving relationships with religious neighbors.

Drawing from the work of Peggy McIntosh on white privilege, Warren Blumenfeld describes Christian privilege as the "seemingly invisible, unearned, and largely unacknowledged" benefits that many Christians enjoy in the United States, which "confers dominance on Christians while subordinating members of other faith communities as well as non-believers."[10] There are numerous ways in which Christian privilege is manifested in this country. One example is the staggering level of choice available to Christians when it comes to worship options: In all but the tiniest of communities, Christians wanting to attend church have so many options that they can select a house of worship based on any number of criteria. Another example of privilege that Christians enjoy but rarely notice comes in the ways in which our society, our schools, and our workplaces structure time. The standard work week allows "Christians the opportunity to worship without conflicting with their work schedules," notes Blumenfeld.[11] Similarly, K-12 and university calendars schedule vacations around Christmas and Easter, ensuring that school won't conflict with family and religious gatherings coinciding with those Christian holidays. Such examples help to "normalize" Christianity while "marginalizing those who do not believe or [who] practice a different faith," says Ellen Fairchild. "This normalizing effect is then used to argue that the United States is a Christian nation, and therefore Christians in some way deserve the benefits afforded them."[12]

These and other examples help demonstrate that Christian privilege exists in America, yet many Christians not only fail to recognize their privileged status but even maintain that their experiences challenge this notion altogether. Reporting on a national survey that he and his colleagues conducted, Wuthnow notes that evangelical Christians feel "embattled."[13] In part, this feeling stems from a changing culture and the uncertainties that inevitably accompany change. By many measures, "Christianity is quickly losing its position of cultural influence. We are no longer the ones in charge, and we don't know what to do about it."[14]

Thus it's no surprise that 92 percent of American evangelicals surveyed by sociologist Christian Smith and his colleagues believe that "American Christians face widespread opposition and prejudice from the secular world."[15] And there is some support for this perspective. Smith notes that "many nonevangelicals [seem to] view evangelical Christians with deep suspicion, as enemies of freedom and democracy."[16] Recognizing this, many religious conservatives say that they "do not feel welcome in the places of public discourse."[17] The feeling that evangelicals aren't welcome is reinforced every time a so-called spokesperson for evangelical Christianity says something offensive and the ensuing media coverage perpetuates the notion that Christian intolerance should be criticized and confronted, which in turn leads Christians to believe that Christianity is under attack. And, note Blumenfeld and Jaekel, even attempts to investigate Christian privilege make some Christians feel that Christianity itself is being condemned.[18]

Counterexamples to Christian privilege can also be found in many American colleges and universities, where evangelical college students "report feeling stereotyped and ostracized on campus" by classmates and some professors.[19] They indicate that they feel "marginalized," "somewhat outside of the mainstream ideologically."[20] Alyssa Bryant Rockenbach describes these students' response as one of "unease"—because of their knowledge of negative stereotypes of Christians and because "their stance on moral absolutes often distance[s] evangelical students from their peers on campus."[21]

Christian privilege can be an obstacle to meaningful relationships with persons of different faith traditions when it fosters an

attitude of superiority that makes it difficult for us to recognize the
goodness in other religious traditions. At the same time, many
Christians fail to recognize the religious privilege they have in society, identifying instead as marginalized or even threatened. Subsequently the "seeming contradiction between privilege and sense
of marginalization" leaves some Christians with an ambiguous
sense of their social status.[22] Complicating the picture further,
argues Sheryl Kujawa-Holbrook, is the fact that our failure to acknowledge the aspects of Christian privilege that do still exist keeps
us from understanding why some religious groups mistrust or even
dread Christians.[23] We must be willing to listen to those who see
the Christian privilege that we perhaps can't (because we naturally
focus on times when we feel marginalized). When we do listen,
we'll be forced to acknowledge that Christians are "not as welcoming as we would like to believe."[24]

Both positions, privileged or marginalized, can perpetuate the
perception that a primary responsibility of Christians is to defend
Christianity against all other secular and religious traditions. Taking
a defensive stance, however, fosters hostility rather than love. This
is particularly problematic when we employ hostility in order "to
make and keep our identities strong."[25]

According to McLaren, the view that strong Christian commitment requires opposition to other faiths is rooted in part in
Christianity's history in the West. Just three hundred years after the
birth of Christ, Constantine converted to Christianity, fought a
battle for control of the empire in the name of Christ, and estab-
lished a connection between the Christian faith and the centers of
political power in the West that lasted for centuries. Considering
the implications of Constantine's famous inscription of the words
"Conquer by this" on the image of a cross, McLaren writes that
such a history seems to "support an oppositional identity where
'we' are the virtuous ones, the victims, the defenders of truth, the

peacemakers, and 'they' are the aggressors, the invaders, the heretics, the evil ones."[26] Following Constantine's legacy, notes Carl Braaten, Christians have not only seen other religions as false, with nothing of value in them, but believers in these non-Christian religions have been (at times literally) "subject to obliteration."[27]

In his studies of American evangelicals, Smith similarly finds evidence of the oppositional identity that McLaren describes. Evangelicalism, says Smith, "flourishes on difference, engagement, tension, conflict, and threat."[28] Smith's research reveals that evangelicals frequently draw sharp distinctions between themselves and others, both within Christianity and the world at large. Such an oppositional identity, in combination with both Christian privilege and various societal critiques of Christianity, leads to much confusion and ambiguity for Christians living today in a religiously pluralistic society.

At the same time, though, Christians need to stop allowing the complexity of our own social status to become a barrier to loving our neighbors well. Instead, we need to listen to and build relationships with persons from other religions—who themselves are often marginalized in American society. As Thomas Ogletree puts it, "We need to give special weight and care to those meaning-worlds which are not normally taken seriously in the social interactions within which we participate from day to day."[29] This requires courage and commitment.

AMBIGUITY AND FEAR

The ambiguous social status in which many Christians find themselves today—simultaneously privileged and embattled—opens up the possibility for either fear or love. We foster fear when we build our identity as Christians around our efforts to stand firm against religious neighbors who aren't "us." If we're to find a way to live out the command to love our religious neighbors, however, we must

learn to analyze and address our fears. Imagine how our perspectives on Christian identity might change if instead of Constantine's
slogan, "Conquer by this," our primary identity was "Serve by this,"
"Reconcile around this," "Embrace like this," "Trust like this," or
"Love like this."[30]

Fear is a dominant trend in our culture today that limits the
degree to which we're willing to love. Americans are often afraid
of others whose looks, votes, or beliefs mark them as "different."
We tend to fear that the world will change in directions we don't
want it to go. We fear that our own lives might have to change to
accommodate others. We no longer trust each other, and our
rates of community engagement have been declining for decades.[31] Biblically, however, we're reminded that fear shouldn't
be our default response to the world around us, "for God has not
given us a spirit of fear and timidity, but of power, love, and self-
discipline" (2 Tim 1:7). We're also told that love is the antidote to
fear. As 1 John 4:18 states, "Such love has no fear, because perfect
love expels all fear."

Expelling fear is important if we hope to love our neighbors as
ourselves. Particularly when it comes to issues related to faith,
fear can easily get in the way because "religious positions touch
the core of our identity. When we're pressed to admit the validity
of multiple viewpoints, many of us feel as if we're turning our back
on God."[32] So instead of interacting with our religious neighbors—
or even with Christians who worship differently than we do—
many of us simply choose whatever place of worship feels most
comfortable, leaving for a different congregation when we encounter disagreements or differences. But when we avoid engaging others because we fear vulnerability and discomfort, we're
failing to love our neighbors.

Ultimately we must choose how we see and interact with those
who believe differently from us. We can use our strong faith

commitments to promote hostility and fear, or we can allow our strong faith commitments to promote the best features of Christianity—love and peace. If we choose fear, developing a self-understanding that's based largely on "who we are in relation to an enemy," this approach "promotes a mentality of us versus them, us apart from them, us instead of them, us without them, us over them, us using them, us in spite of them, us oppressed by them, or us occupying them."[33] On the other hand, if we choose love over fear, we open ourselves to becoming strong and benevolent believers. This switch from hostility to solidarity actually puts us more in line with the central teachings of Christianity. It affirms the core identity of Christians as those who love rather than fear—an identity the Gospels illustrate vividly, most notably in the parable of the lost son and the parable of the good Samaritan.

THE PARABLE OF THE LOST SON: CHALLENGING MISPLACED NOTIONS OF PURITY

The parable of the lost son, found in Luke 15:11-32, is the third in a series of stories Jesus tells about losing—and then joyously finding—what's been lost.[34] In this familiar parable, the attitudes and actions of two brothers reveal that each is lost in his own way. The younger brother, wanting to try out life on his own, asks for his inheritance early. Equipped with these funds, he takes a trip "to a distant land, and there he wasted all his money in wild living" (Lk 15:13). His resources utterly depleted, this prodigal son (for whom the story is most commonly named) decides to return home, admit his disgrace, and throw himself on his father's mercy. The father, however, "filled with love and compassion . . . ran to his son, embraced him, and kissed him," giving him an extravagant welcome (Lk 15:20-24). In thinking about this story we're often guided to see the loving grace of the father, a God figure who showers grace on even those who've spent much time far away from him.

The older brother, however, is also lost—but he doesn't realize it. When the misbehaving younger brother goes "to a distant land," the dutiful older brother remains home with his father, acting as a good, responsible son. Returning home at the end of a day working in the fields, the older brother hears the music and dancing that is part of the party hosted by his father to celebrate the wayward younger brother's safe return (Lk 15:25-27). This news angers the older brother so much that he refuses to even enter the house, despite his father's coming outside and begging him to come in and join them (Lk 15:28). Why is the older brother so angry? Because he feels that his own hard work for the father "all these years" hasn't ever been acknowledged, in sharp contrast to the celebration over the prodigal's return (Lk 15:29-30).

This parable is well known. Many of us are even familiar with the interpretation that this story is as much about the older brother's unwillingness to embrace the younger son as it is about the prodigal's rebellion. When we view it this way, we can see Jesus telling the parable to challenge the "older brothers"—those of us who seek to be deeply and unwaveringly committed to our faith over the course of our lifetimes—to be more welcoming. McLaren makes this point when he notes that both brothers in this story "suffer from an identity crisis."[35] The younger son's crisis, thumbing his nose at his father by leaving home and squandering the inheritance on loose living and coming home in shame, is easy to see. But the older son's crisis is particularly instructive for those who want to

> You can't maintain hostility against "the other" without also withdrawing from the father who loves both you and the other as beloved children.
> **BRIAN McLAREN**

learn to be better religious neighbors. In his harsh and angry words near the end of the story, we see that "you can't maintain hostility against 'the other' without also withdrawing from the father who loves both you and the other as beloved children."[36]

This lesson can also be seen in the scriptural context of where the parable is placed in Luke's Gospel. Luke 15 begins with religious leaders "complain[ing] that he was associating with . . . such sinful people—even eating with them!" (Lk 15:2). McLaren humorously emphasizes the contemporary relevance of this context by offering his own "update" of the scene:

> Now all the Muslims and Buddhists, New Agers and agnostics were coming near to listen to him. And the radio preachers and heresy hunters were grumbling and saying, "This fellow welcomes non-Christians and eats with them." So he told them this parable . . . [37]

As this parable—particularly the older brother's hostility—helps emphasize, too often Christians believe that the best way to live as faithful followers of Christ is through so-called "purity," making sure not to associate too closely with those whose beliefs are opposed to the gospel. But this isn't the message we see in how Jesus lived his life. And it's not the message we're taught about the older brother in the parable of the lost son. Why is the older brother rebuked? Because of his refusal to love, to welcome, to show hospitality to his "impure" younger brother.

THE PARABLE OF THE GOOD SAMARITAN:
CHALLENGING RELIGIOUS PATERNALISM

We know the two-part biblical command: to love God with our whole being (heart, soul, strength, and mind) and to love our neighbor as we love ourselves. And we've also heard the story Jesus told to help clarify what it means to love our neighbor—the parable of the good Samaritan.

In this story, found in Luke 10:29-37, an unidentified man traveling alone was "attacked by bandits" who "stripped him of his clothes, beat him up, and left him half dead beside the road" (Lk 10:30). As the injured man lay there, at least three different people walked by. The first, a priest, "crossed to the other side of the road" in order to avoid the man; the second, a "Temple assistant," didn't utterly avoid the man but "walked over and looked at him lying there" before continuing on his journey (Lk 10:31-32). Then a "despised Samaritan came along." Instead of abandoning the injured man, as the two religious leaders had done, the Samaritan helped—taking his own time, energy, and money to do so (Lk 10:33-35).

Those who've grown up anywhere near a church have heard numerous Sunday school lessons and sermons based on this story. Perhaps you even helped your teacher move a figure on the flannelgraph board to help it come alive while she told this story. Or you might have been able to learn helpfulness by sticking Band-Aids on a drawing of a hurt person. You might have been challenged to focus on the hypocrisy of the religious leaders in the story, since they don't stop to help the injured man. You might similarly have been challenged to consider that the hero of the story, a Samaritan, would have been viewed by many of Jesus' first followers as a racial outsider.

These readings of the story are all supportable, of course. But we also need to reflect on the possible implications for interfaith relations. After all, Samaritans weren't just racial outsiders—they would also have been seen by Jesus' Jewish followers as religious outsiders, despised for their heretical beliefs and hated for the long history of animosity between Jews and Samaritans. In Jesus' day, notes biblical scholar Amy-Jill Levine, this animosity was so great that if Jewish hearers of the story were to imagine themselves as the injured man, they would certainly "balk at the idea of receiving Samaritan aid. They might have thought, 'I'd rather die than acknowledge that one from that group saved me.'"[38]

If this story were merely about the importance of helping those in need, Jesus could have had the hero be another Jewish religious leader with better priorities than those who abandoned the man without assisting him. Or he could have had the hero be a farmer or carpenter or fisherman—someone like any number of Jesus' regular followers. But he didn't. The hero of this story is a religious enemy who "felt compassion" for the injured man, "going over to him" to provide comfort and medical attention (Lk 10:33-34). The Samaritan even uses his own animal to transport the man, spends his own time to care for the man, and spends his own money to provide further assistance.[39]

Jesus challenges religious paternalism by choosing a religious outsider—a heretic—as this story's hero. Religious paternalism is the perspective that we are the ones who know and believe the correct theology and who act accordingly to the benefit of the "unfortunates" and "the lost" we encounter. Jesus turns all of that upside down in this story. Not only is the Samaritan the one who shows love and kindness toward the hurt man, but Jesus is clearly saying to his hearers that even religious leaders and theological experts have something to learn from a religious outsider about "how to interpret and obey the law" and demonstrating how they themselves "need to change in order to be counted among the neighborly."[40] Similarly, Jeannine Hill Fletcher notes that "in answering the fundamental question of what pattern brings life, Jesus reaches outside of his own community and raises the 'other,' the despised, as the model to follow."[41]

For these reasons, Joshua Graves observes that this parable provides "the paradigmatic lens for Christian leaders to participate in dialogue, shared ministry, and deep appreciation for our American Muslim neighbors. If taken seriously, this one biblical text would revolutionize the way we see, live, act, and think. Christians would begin to view their Muslim neighbors with new eyes."[42] How can we hear this all-too-familiar parable in a way that helps us heed its message and recapture the force it might have had for its original audience? Here's how we might "update" the story:

> Traveling through a dangerous part of town, a man was mugged and savagely beaten. A few minutes later, an evangelical pastor came upon the unconscious man. Knowing this area to be dangerous—and already late for an appointment—the pastor hurried past. When a seminary professor happened on the scene, she too kept right on driving.
>
> But a Muslim immigrant did more than just look at the man, as the religious leaders had done: He *noticed* him.[43] Moved with compassion, the Muslim stopped to bandage the man's wounds and comfort him. Then he put the man in his own car, brought him to a motel, and took care of him. The next day he took out his wallet and gave all the cash he had to the motel manager, saying, "Take care of him, and whatever else you spend, I'll repay you when I come back this way."

In telling this story, Jesus helps us see what it looks like to be a good neighbor—to engage in neighborly actions that demonstrate mercy and compassion. He helps us see that questions about who is (or who isn't) a "neighbor" are irrelevant: *"Be a neighbor*—no more questions or answers required."[44] And since we unfortunately need such reminders, this parable also demonstrates that "God works in and through *them* as well as *us.*"[45]

What we learn from both of these parables is that interfaith partnerships and interactions don't compromise our identity as Christians. Rather, they flow directly from our faithfulness to Christ. Rather than continuing to define ourselves by who we're not, taking a combative stance toward our religious neighbors, Christians ought to define ourselves by who we are: people who seek to love the Lord our God and to love our neighbors. As we see through the neighborly actions of the "heretical" Samaritan, "To speak of loving God and loving neighbor does not require theological precision," suggests Levine. "Loving God and loving neighbor . . . [simply] need to be enacted."[46] Rather than experiencing conflict within our Christian identity, we live out our Christian faith by loving our neighbors, even—maybe even particularly—our religious neighbors. This isn't a paternalistic love but a welcoming and hospitable love, a love committed to our own religious identity yet also willing to respect the identity of religious others. In the next chapter we develop a model for interfaith engagement that helps us balance genuine commitment to our own Christian faith with love and respect for persons committed to other religions.

> To speak of loving God and loving neighbor does not require theological precision. Loving God and loving neighbor . . . [simply] need to be enacted.
> AMY-JILL LEVINE

TALK ABOUT IT

• Think about Christians you know well who demonstrate a strong commitment to their faith. Do they tend to be hostile or benevolent to other religions? Why do you think this is the case? Do you think benevolence can be an appropriate extension of a strong commitment to Christianity?

• In what ways do Christians on your campus or in your community experience privilege? Are there any ways in which they are also marginalized?

• What, if anything, do you fear about interfaith engagement?

How might the parables of the good Samaritan and the lost son address those fears?

GIVE IT A TRY

Chapter seven contains many practical ideas for implementing the ideas in this book. Try one of the role-playing exercises described on pages 146-47.

YOU DON'T HAVE TO WATER DOWN YOUR IDENTITY

Amber Hacker, vice president of operations and communications, Interfaith Youth Core

There's a moment that always happens to me when I meet someone new and I'm asked what I do for a living: I look down at my watch and calculate whether I have enough time to explain that I work for an interfaith organization—and what that means for me as a born-again Christian.

I grew up in a Baptist church in the Piedmont Triad area of North Carolina. I made my profession of faith when I was nine years old by asking Jesus to come into my heart and hopping into our church's beloved "dunking booth" to be baptized. I'm a born-again Christian who does interfaith work for a living at an organization in Chicago called Interfaith Youth Core, which seeks to build a movement of people from all faiths and traditions who are working together to change the world, and I've been at it now for almost nine years. When I tell my Christian brothers and sisters what I do for a living, I get a range of reactions: furrowed brows, polite head nods, enthusiasm, and challenging, critical statements about my chosen career path.

I find there are numerous misconceptions about interfaith work—that it means everyone should be a part of one big religion or that it implies that everyone believes the same thing but are taking different paths. Neither of these definitions is true to me, and neither describes the interfaith movement I belong to. To me, interfaith cooperation means we have a basic respect for religious and nonreligious identities, that we build on that respect to form mutually inspiring relationships, and that we come together based on our shared values to serve our communities. It means that you don't have to water down your identity to come to the table of interfaith cooperation—whether you're an evangelical Christian, Muslim, Hindu, Jew, or atheist, you don't have to compromise what you believe (or what you don't believe) to engage in interfaith work.

Some members of my Christian community have expressed concern that I'll be converted away from Christianity if I engage in interfaith efforts. But interfaith work has only strengthened my identity as a Christian. In my work, many non-Christians have asked me questions about my faith story and different tenets of my tradition that have challenged me to go back to my Christian community to get answers. I've had numerous opportunities to share my testimony and what Jesus means to me. Furthermore, engaging with difference and learning about other traditions hasn't made me want to convert or let go of my faith—in fact, quite the opposite has happened.

When I learned that my Muslim friend Usra prays five times a day, I felt called to look at my own prayer life and think about how I could make it a more regular practice. When I found out my Jewish friend Josh fasted for Yom Kippur, I was inspired to look at what a fasting practice might look like in my tradition. When I spoke with my atheist friend Adam who doesn't believe in God but believes this is the only life that we get and we have an obligation to serve others, his passion and commitment to humanity calls me to think about what it means to bring the kingdom of heaven here on earth (Mt 13).

Some members of my Christian community have expressed concern that interfaith work isn't biblical. In actuality, there are many arguments for interfaith cooperation. Perhaps the most salient one for me is the parable of the good Samaritan (Lk 10:25-37). Jesus tells that parable in response to an expert in the Scriptures who wants to know how Jesus defines the "neighbor" we are called to love. In the original language, the Greek word used for "love" is *agape*, which means the highest form of love—the same kind of love that God has for all people. And who is our neighbor that we are called to love? It is the Samaritan, who showed compassion and mercy to the Jewish man who had been robbed and left for dead.

At the time Jews and Samaritans were two different religious groups harboring deep animosity toward one another. In his story Jesus emphasizes the importance of caring for your neighbor, especially when that person is from a different background and tradition from your own. That person you disagree with the most—someone you even despise? That's your neighbor. That's who you are called to love. Engaging in interfaith work gives me that opportunity to love and serve alongside a community of people from different backgrounds. I may have deep theological and political disagreements with many of these folks. But I have a biblical calling to love them as my neighbors.

> I do interfaith work not despite the fact that I'm a Christian, but I do it because I am a Christian. To me, being a Christian and an interfaith leader aren't mutually exclusive but are mutually enriching.

I believe that Jesus is the way, the truth, and the life (Jn 14:6). I am a born-again Christian. I am an interfaith leader. I do interfaith work not despite the fact that I'm a Christian, but because I am a Christian. To me, being a Christian and an interfaith leader aren't mutually exclusive but are mutually enriching. I am a better Christ-follower because I engage with those who are different from me.

4

A Model for
Interfaith Engagement

We know we ought to love our religious neighbors, but how should we go about it? In responding to religious diversity, some people see tolerance as the primary goal, urging us to recognize and respect the other's right to hold a view different from our own. By taking the tolerant approach we may be able to establish civic harmony and keep religious differences from leading to violence. And because tolerance doesn't require us to really engage or wrestle with other views, it's often valued as a low-risk and comfortable path toward coexistence.

A second possible stance toward religious difference is affirmation. Affirmation goes beyond tolerance to pursue meaningful interaction with persons who believe differently. For the sake of understanding and caring for the other, this model suggests that we try to see the world entirely through the other's eyes and affirm that view. In this model we refrain from asserting our own views so we don't offend the other person or undermine her views. Not only does this approach promote harmony, it can also foster empathy and genuine concern for persons from other religious traditions.

In this chapter we take a closer look at both of these approaches and ultimately argue that neither is adequate for healthy interfaith engagement.[1] While both paths—tolerance and affirmation—have important strengths, we believe they also limit our pursuit of a healthy love of our religious neighbors. So instead we advocate a middle path that we call inclusion, characterized by mutual understanding and genuine dialogue with our religious neighbors. This model, informed by the work of Martin Buber and Miroslav Volf, allows us to come to a clearer and more accurate understanding of other religious traditions and thus to build constructive, ongoing friendships with persons who believe differently. In addition, this model doesn't require bracketing off or even denying our own views. Instead the path of inclusion actually strengthens our religious identity and faith commitments.

> **Inclusion promotes a shared reality where all partners in the dialogue come to understand each other's position, even if they don't agree with it, and build a meaningful relationship despite their differences.**

THE PATH OF INCLUSION

Successful interfaith engagement between persons with deep faith commitments requires forging a path where we can express our own beliefs and perspectives while at the same time respectfully listening to and seeking to understand the beliefs of others. Inclusion promotes a shared reality where all partners in the dialogue come to understand each other's position, even if they don't agree with it, and build a meaningful relationship despite their differences.[2] An inclusive model of dialogue, therefore, accepts the strengths of tolerance and of affirmation. By following the inclusive path, we seek to love the other as neighbor, going deeper than mere tolerance but not going as far as full affirmation. In order to understand this concept more fully, let's consider how the idea of inclusion emerges from a theory of self and community in the work of both Martin Buber and Miroslav Volf.

Genuinely inclusive dialogue. Our use of the word *inclusion* comes from Buber's work on the essential role of genuine dialogue in cultivating and maintaining meaningful relationships between persons and communities. As Buber explains, genuine dialogue occurs "where each of the participants really has in mind the other or others in their present and particular being and turns to them with the intention of establishing a living mutual relation."[3] In genuine dialogue, the encounter between self and other forms a living foundation for meaningful relationship and community, even if each person holds very different beliefs. Describing the goal of genuine dialogue, Buber writes, "What is called for is not 'neutrality' but solidarity . . . and mutuality, living reciprocity; not effacing the boundaries between [people] . . . , but communal recognition of the common reality and . . . [our] common responsibility."[4]

Buber's concept of genuine dialogue is rooted in his famous distinction between I-It and I-Thou.[5] These terms describe two possible ways of being in relation to the world, other human beings, and God. According to Buber, the self is always in relation to others—it's not a question of *whether* the self will relate but rather of *how* she will relate. In I-Thou relations, the self turns toward the other, confirming the other as a partner, seeking to transcend the distance that separates self and other. The self neither subsumes the other into herself nor is she subsumed; rather, the self and the other exist together in a world of relation characterized by solidarity and genuine fellowship.

Buber often describes what takes place between I and Thou as genuine dialogue, because in genuine dialogue, the self and the other reciprocally acknowledge and confirm each other's existence.

Buber maintains that there are different degrees of genuine dialogue, depending on the degree of inclusion and mutuality present. He defines the elements of inclusion as, "first, a relation . . . between two persons, second an event experienced by them in common, in which at least one of them actually participates, and third, the fact that this one person, without forfeiting anything of the felt reality of his activity, at the same time lives through the common event from the standpoint of the other."[6] When two individuals recognize and affirm each other with at least some degree of mutuality, genuine dialogue is present. So any form of genuine dialogue must involve an attitude of openness by both partners to include the other in the sphere of commonality between them.

The degree of inclusion varies. For example, a disagreement where both participants recognize the other's perspective as sharing in the truth but do so without relativizing the truth is a form of genuine dialogue. It's limited, however, because it's not completely inclusive. This is because, while each person abstractly acknowledges the personhood of the other, they don't seek to experience the life of the other from the other's perspective. In contrast to this sort of relationship with little inclusion, Buber suggests that a friendship provides the most "concrete and mutual" experience of inclusion.[7] As Buber envisions friendship, two persons reciprocally recognize and include each other as whole persons, give themselves freely to the discussion, and don't seek to impose their ideas upon each other. There is "meeting" between self and other; something "happens" between them. This implies that the self and other are mutually impacted by the relationship. In Buber's words, "I become through my relation to the Thou; as I become I, I say Thou. All real living is meeting."[8]

Like Buber, Volf's view of the self as formed through relationships also helps us see how a person might balance her own belief commitments while remaining open to and challenged by the perspectives of others. Volf writes, "I am who I am in relation to the other. . . . The other must be part of who I am as I will to be myself. As a result, a tension between the self and the other is built into the very desire for identity."[9] This tension is present because, in relation to others, we're "both separated and connected, both distinct and related."[10] Such a view of the self leads Volf to critique two possible approaches to dealing with difference. Unbounded affirmation is both impossible and undesirable because we can't remain ourselves unless we maintain some sense of boundary between self and other (separate and distinct). Mere tolerance is inadequate because we can't become ourselves unless we allow ourselves to develop deep bonds with others that will shape us (connected and related).

Instead, Volf urges us to see that each of us is "enriched by otherness," shaped in various ways by our interactions.[11] Yet as we welcome others and seek to be enriched by contact with them, we aren't simply sponges that soak up all possible influences. Thus we approach interfaith engagement in ways similar to Buber's image of genuine dialogue and inclusion—listening generously, working to understand and willing to be touched by the faith stories of others, practicing the sort of hospitality that we described in chapter two. At the same time, recognizing that we're shaped by our faith just as others are shaped by theirs, we don't shy away from telling our own stories.

Inclusive dialogue as embrace. Inclusive dialogue seeks to break down boundaries and develop deep relationships with other people and with things that others have created, such as texts and works of art. For such a relationship to develop, one must be a "receptive beholder," approaching others with an attitude of "mutuality, openness, [and] listening, . . . [a] 'sense of wonder' and 'astonishment.'"[12] This requires a willingness to engage the other in a manner that pursues mutual understanding and may actually end in a changed view. While one seeks to cultivate openness and receptiveness, at the same time there's a recognition of the distance between beings, acknowledging the important boundaries that differentiate us.[13]

Volf uses the metaphor of a physical embrace to capture the essence of this inclusive view of interfaith engagement. An embrace, says Volf, has four elements: "opening the arms, waiting, closing the arms, and opening them again."[14] The first movement in an embrace—opening the arms—signals that "I do not want to be by myself only."[15] It demonstrates a willingness to embrace the other and shows that others are seen as potentially enriching friends rather than as potentially diminishing enemies. This movement shows that I have "created space in myself for the other to come in and that I have made a movement out of myself so as to enter the space created by the other."[16] In creating this space, open arms also issue an invitation to the other to enter. After opening one's arms, the willingness to embrace is next signaled by waiting to see if the invitation has been accepted. This waiting reminds both parties that there's no coercion involved in an embrace: "Each has the right to refuse."[17]

The third movement—closed arms—requires a "soft touch," where the other isn't crushed and where the inviter's boundaries of self remain intact as well. Closed arms are a sign, says Volf, that "I want the other to become a part of me while I at the same time maintain my own identity. By becoming part of me, the other enriches me. In a mutual embrace, none remains the same because each enriches the other, yet both remain true to their genuine selves."[18]

After the embrace has occurred, the arms open again, thus releasing as well as inviting the other to return.[19] An embracing approach to interfaith engagement isn't merely "a false pluralism of approving pats on the back," says Volf. "Since truth matters, . . . we

will . . . engage others over differences and incompatibilities, so as
to both learn from and teach others."[20]

> **In a mutual embrace, none remains the
> same because each enriches the other, yet
> both remain true to their genuine selves.**
> MIROSLAV VOLF

The four movements of Volf's metaphor of embrace involve an
alternation between seeing "from here" and "from there."[21] It's
natural to see "from here," says Volf. This means seeing "from our
own perspective, guided by our own values and interests that are
shaped by the overlapping cultures and traditions we inhabit."[22] It
involves reading "the beliefs and practices of others through the
lenses of our own tradition."[23] Of course this step is essential. But
it's not sufficient. We also must seek to see "from there," inverting
our perspective in order to "enter sympathetically into others' efforts to interpret their scripture."[24] We listen to them tell their "own
story about who they see themselves to be."[25] And we listen as they
describe their perceptions of us.[26]

The hospitality we practice when we see "from here" as well as
"from there" is crucial to interfaith interactions. Such an attitude
helps us see and affirm commonalities between religions and
among people, an important part of bridge-building. But we must
not limit ourselves to finding commonalities: What's most important about each religion, notes Volf, is "the particular configu-
ration of its elements, which may overlap with, differ from or con-
tradict elements of other religions."[27] Thus, participants in interfaith
dialogue don't need to leave their own faith commitments at the
door when they enter into conversation. Each participant speaks
from her own position within her faith tradition.

Buber recognized this. When asked to speak a language more "universal" than that shaped by his own Jewish tradition, he responded, "In order to speak to the world what I have heard I am not bound to step into the street. I may remain in the door of my ancestral house."[28] Volf recognized this as well. For him, speaking as a Christian means "to give voice to the Christian faith in its concreteness, whether what is said overlaps with, differs from, or contradicts what people speaking in a Jewish or Muslim voice are saying."[29]

Inclusion and the common good. Buber uses the pronoun *we* to describe the relationship of genuinely inclusive dialogue, signifying that the partners in the conversation have transcended the limiting distinction between *us* and *them*, without becoming entirely subsumed into the perspective of the other. The meeting between self and other, as we, in inclusive dialogue provides a constructive model for addressing religious diversity. The goal of such dialogue is the relationship itself, the opportunity it provides to be confirmed by the other as well as to experience the other's side—to confirm rather than convert or coerce.

The goal of such dialogue is the relationship itself.

Buber describes a community marked by inclusion as "no union of the like-minded but a genuine living together of . . . [those] of differing minds. Community is the overcoming of otherness in living unity."[30] The sort of community Buber envisions could certainly include persons of different faiths. Buber was himself an advocate of shared community between Jews and Arabs in Palestine, and as such he reflects this commitment to inclusion in his own life. In a letter to Mahatma Gandhi, Buber acknowledges the challenge of uniting these two

groups. Recognizing that the claims of both Jews and Arabs are
rooted in foundationally different views, making it impossible to
adjudicate between them, Buber writes that it is

> our duty to understand and to honor the claim which is op-
> posed to ours and to endeavor to reconcile both claims. . . .
> We have been and still are convinced that it must be pos-
> sible to find some compromise. . . . Where there is faith and
> love, a solution may be found even to what appears to be a
> tragic opposition.[31]

Buber acknowledges both the difficulty of inclusion and the possibility that it won't succeed. He notes, however, that we must not
allow ourselves to be the reason why such a project fails. It's possible for the other to neglect to recognize me as Thou or to leave
the relationship of meeting between us, but I'm responsible to
remain continually open to the possibility of genuine dialogue.

> **Seek to live with others in a manner
> that maintains both commitment
> to personal belief and genuine
> respect for the other's perspective.**

When applying the models of inclusion found in both Buber and
Volf to the topic of interfaith engagement, it's important to recognize that the goal is friendship and healthy civic partnership.
Buber doesn't present a theory for how to evaluate the truth of
competing views, nor does he argue that the truth of one's view is
irrelevant. Rather, his priority is this: Seek to live with others in a
manner that maintains both commitment to personal belief and
genuine respect for the other's perspective, for "the truth of a
world-view is not proved in the clouds but in lived life."[32]

The Danger of Tolerance

To many in a pluralistic society, tolerance may sound like a safer and more realistic goal than Buber's inclusion or Volf's embrace. The path of tolerance suggests that we remain neutral on matters of religion so that we neither openly endorse nor reject beliefs and persons who are different from us. Tolerance typically takes one of two forms. It can recognize the other's right to believe differently while avoiding interaction with them. Or it can politely limit interaction with the other to shared beliefs and values. Both approaches to tolerance seek to avoid potentially uncomfortable disagreements and thus often appear to be open and respectful forms of interaction. But, ultimately, both forms of tolerance fail to encourage genuine love of neighbor.

The first form of tolerance—pursuing peace through neutrality—involves drawing a sharp divide between our public and private selves. Public disturbance is avoided by keeping people's religious identities private, with the goal of creating a neutral public sphere. This perspective is evident in France's 2011 law banning women from wearing *niqab*, full veil, in public. Similarly, in American higher education, the common assumption that classrooms should be religiously neutral often leads religion to be removed from the classroom altogether. And in political philosophy, there's a long history of those who argue that religion has no place in the public sphere because in such contexts it is more divisive than constructive.[33] Richard Rorty provides a common articulation of this view, arguing that democratic societies should "think of themselves as having exchanged tolerance for an assurance that believers would leave their religion at home when discussing political questions in public."[34]

While we don't advocate the "peace through neutrality" approach, we do recognize that this version of tolerance is often motivated by a desire to prevent any one religious perspective from

being forced on others. For example, requiring all citizens to say a
Christian prayer at a public event or allowing only Christian Scriptures to be read in public wouldn't be appropriate in a pluralistic
democracy such as ours. Respect for all—including those in the
religious minority—needs to be practiced.

Buber draws from his own childhood experience to show the
harm that can result from one religious perspective being privileged over another. As a child Buber was one of only a few Jewish
students enrolled in a school made up primarily of Christians. Each
morning the teacher had the students stand and recite a compulsory common prayer while the Jewish students stood in silence.
According to Buber, the difficulty in this situation was not that the
Christians in the room lacked tolerance, but rather that there was
no genuine acknowledgement of his religious identity. He explains
that the "obligatory daily standing in the room" was worse than an
overt act of intolerance would have been. He felt like he and his
fellow Jewish students were treated as "compulsory guests, having
to participate as a thing in a sacral event in which no dram of my
person could or would take part."[35]

At least two significant problems emerge when tolerance is
pursued through neutrality. First, merely respecting the other's
right to hold different beliefs doesn't create a meaningful and loving
relationship, because no real attempt is made to understand and
interact with the other's perspective. This limitation is often revealed when religious persons protest the strict separation between
public and private beliefs, arguing that they can't separate their
identities in this manner. For example, many Muslim women in
France see the so-called neutrality laws as a form of religious discrimination. Similarly, many Christians in America react against
the removal of prayer from public spaces. And deeply religious students from many traditions often find it challenging to bracket off
their religious beliefs when discussing various academic topics.

While peaceful coexistence without imposing one's religious tradition on others is an important goal, neutrality isn't the best path toward peace. The path of inclusion provides the opportunity to pursue mutual understanding that not only respects difference but encourages open and ongoing dialogue about those differences for the sake of understanding and civic solidarity.

Another problem with the neutral approach to religious difference is this: Most religious persons don't perceive neutrality as neutral. Instead, neutrality asserts secularism as the preferred language of the public sphere. And this privileging of the secular or nonreligious can actually harm religious persons, because it doesn't allow them to fully engage in public life.

In order to avoid this type of harm and acknowledge the religious identity of the other, a second form of tolerance is often employed. In this case, peace is sought through a watered-down form of coexistence, where we navigate religious differences by doing nothing more than celebrating what we share in common. For example, we might host an event on campus where we read texts from different religious traditions but not actually discuss why the various traditions hold these beliefs, or we might only ever consider texts with similar meanings and never discuss the important differences among religious traditions. In either case we fail to engage religious difference in a deep (and perhaps at times uncomfortable) way.

Unfortunately, this second type of tolerance also fails to fully embrace and acknowledge the religious identity of our neighbors. A cursory knowledge of other religions that fails to go beyond lowest common denominators doesn't foster real mutual understanding. We must be willing to consider differences in religious belief and practice—even if such consideration leads to deep disagreement. Taking differences seriously, and maintaining a meaningful relationship in spite of them, is what the path of inclusion offers that the path of tolerance doesn't. We're capable of more than affirming commonalities, and pushing ourselves to love our neighbors instead of simply tolerating them provides the firmer foundation we need in order to address today's civic challenges.

> **Taking differences seriously, and maintaining a meaningful relationship in spite of them, is what the path of inclusion offers that the path of tolerance doesn't.**

There are many situations in today's world where religious differences have erupted into violence. In such contexts learning to tolerate others represents progress and can become an initial step toward civic harmony and mutual understanding. But tolerance can't be seen as the ultimate goal, because it doesn't go far enough. Discussions that emphasize tolerance can become little more than monologue that's disguised as dialogue: Because open conflict is avoided, it appears that people are listening to each other, that they're approaching ideas openly.[36] Such a mindset doesn't get at the root of religious violence and disagreement, though, and it doesn't encourage us to see how and whether our own perspectives toward others might be problematic. (In fact, such a mindset may even strengthen negative thoughts and feelings toward others.) Tolerance doesn't acknowledge the many ways in which human selves are interconnected nor the ways in which coming to know is a collaborative venture. Instead tolerance can feed attitudes that distance and objectify.

Tolerance is both inadequate and potentially harmful. While it may succeed temporarily in arresting the "destructive forces of ignorance, fear, and prejudice," it merely provides what Victor Kazanjian and Peter Laurence describe as a "kind of wall between warring parties." This wall may keep people from harming each other, but it does so at a cost. Because the wall of tolerance also separates, it doesn't "allow for learning, growth, or transformation, but ultimately keeps people in a state of suspended ignorance and conflict."[37]

Surface-level coexistence is also problematic because it can lead to an untenable cultural relativism that ultimately weakens the weight of each person's own beliefs. Inclusion on the other hand takes us deeper by revealing the significant beliefs held by different persons. Our most deeply held beliefs, whether similar to or different from another's, get to the core of who we are as persons. In the words of Paul Mendes-Flohr, we can pursue inclusion that "derives its energy from a compelling desire to know and honour the Other, and perhaps at a deeper level, a conviction that the Other, despite his or her difference—and perhaps even because of this difference . . . shares some basic humanity with oneself."[38]

The Danger of Affirmation

In order to build deeper and more meaningful relationships than those that result from mere tolerance, some advocate the route of affirmation. Affirmation is marked by a commitment to go outside of ourselves and see the world through the other's perspective. The approach of affirmation has several benefits, including overcoming either exclusion or a distant neutrality, the potential for building meaningful emotional and intellectual bonds between people, and establishing peace. If, however, affirmation becomes the primary means for going beyond tolerance and isn't balanced with appropriate boundaries, it can amount to what Steven Kepnes describes as "amorphous enmeshment," a collectivity in which personal existence is atrophied.[39] Without appropriate boundaries, affirmation can lead us to feel that we must erase or abandon our own faith commitments for the sake of the other. Inclusion, on the other hand, seeks to balance my commitment to understanding the other with a commitment to openly sharing my own beliefs and values.

The philosophy of Emmanuel Levinas is often used as a framework for the affirmation model of interfaith engagement. Levinas, a Jewish philosopher of Lithuanian birth, was a prisoner of war during World War II who lost most of his relatives in concentration camps. These major life events clearly shape much of his emphasis on our ethical responsibility to recognize and affirm the other.

Levinas's philosophy takes as its starting place an absolute distance between self and other that gives primacy to an ethical view of the relationship over an ontological and epistemological analysis of the relationship. Levinas believes that how I respond to the other is always the most important philosophical issue. In order to protect the other from harm, I have an ethical responsibility to always put the other before myself. In doing this I avoid imposing my view of the truth on her and refrain from reducing her identity to my own perspectives. The separation between us allows her the freedom to have control over her own identity.

Because of this distance between self and other, Levinas doesn't believe that we come to understand ourselves in dialogical relationship with the other, as Buber and Volf believe. Rather, Levinas maintains that the "face" of the other always confronts us first. In this moment "my own efforts to know and so to assimilate the other person are called into question."[40] According to Levinas, the other is ultimately incomprehensible in her otherness; her identity extends beyond the boundaries of what can be contained within my own consciousness.

Levinas's ideas become clearer in the context of living in a religiously pluralistic world. Islamophobia, for example, is a growing problem in the United States and Europe. Often it's fueled by inaccurate representations of what it means to be a practicing Muslim. If a person hasn't had the opportunity to interact meaningfully with many Muslims, he or she may more easily succumb to inflammatory anti-Muslim sentiment. If these false beliefs aren't challenged by genuine interactions with Muslims, fear of the unknown can easily harden into a hatred of the other. The affirmation model attempts to avoid this danger by establishing an ethical responsibility to create opportunities for religious others to speak the truth about their beliefs and practices.

According to Levinas, the other doesn't address a generic self with a generic ethical responsibility. Instead, he or she directly calls to *me*, asking to be acknowledged and affirmed as other than me. This obligation to respond to the other as Other, then, is always prior to any dialogue between us. Thus it's my ethical responsibility to keep the relationship between myself and the other asymmetrical, which means that ethical demands are placed on me that the other isn't obligated to reciprocate. I'm responsible to allow the other to speak, but I can't force her to respond to me. In this way the other isn't put in the uncomfortable position of having to continually defend herself—which many marginalized persons easily tire of doing.

According to Levinas, "Only a being who is responsible for another being can enter into dialogue with it. Responsibility, in the etymological sense of the term, not the mere exchange of words, is what is meant by dialogue."[41] In the context of interfaith engagement, Levinas's emphasis on the ethical over the epistemological implies going beyond merely learning about the other's religion to actually coming to know the other as a person. His model implies that I should seek to see the world as the other sees it, pursuing an understanding of her own view of religion. The tendency is for us to evaluate another religion through our own cultural and religious lenses. But this limits and possibly even distorts the other's beliefs, values, and experiences. So, for Levinas, I should always respond to the other in the manner of a servant, denying my position for the sake of her own position. This perspective prevents me from ever forcing my beliefs, values, and perspectives on the other.

This attitude of asymmetrical servitude initially sounds consistent with the things we had to say in chapter two about hospitality and love of neighbor. But while hospitality is central to loving our religious neighbors, the asymmetrical model of Levinas ultimately fails to achieve the reciprocal partnership between others and ourselves that is necessary in a religiously pluralistic world. In fact, Buber and Levinas argued at length over this very issue. For Levinas, Buber's inclusive model of genuine dialogue places too much responsibility on the other by suggesting that both partners in the dialogue should share the role of speaker and listener. Buber, on the other hand, describes a genuine dialogue between I and Thou attaining its "true greatness and powerfulness" when persons "without a spiritual ground in common . . . still stand over against each other so that each of the two knows and means, recognizes and acknowledges, accepts and confirms the other, even in the severest conflict, as this particular person."[42]

The differences between Buber and Levinas are clearer when we put the philosophical debate back into the context of interfaith dialogue. Robert Gibbs describes a Levinasian approach to interfaith engagement as one in which my sole task is to listen: "I listen, in part, to learn again and again, that I don't know the other person. She is not an object to me, nor is she my equal. She is rather my teacher. One on one, the other is always my teacher."[43] In the asymmetrical path of affirmation, I stay in the role of listener and don't engage as participant, collaborator, partner, or co-teacher. For Buber and Volf, on the other hand, the ideal path is to go further than affirmation. Not only should I listen to and seek to understand the other from her own perspective, I should also seek to cultivate a relationship with her where I can humbly and openly share my own perspectives. In this way our interactions can be mutual instead of one-sided.

It's true that many positive outcomes result from taking the path of affirmation. Like tolerance, affirmation may help foster civic harmony and peace. As Ryan Urbano maintains, if we see each religion as "an Other, a face," seeking to see it "from the perspective of a believer who is a person, a human Other, the tendency towards fundamentalism, dogmatism and violence withers."[44] Unlike tolerance, affirmation promotes genuine interaction with and learning from our religious neighbors. Paul Knitter describes the usefulness of Levinas for interfaith engagement this way: "In the otherness of my religious friend I find differences that I will never be able to include neatly in my limited categories. . . . In the face of the religious other I see or sense the face of the Other that shines within and beyond us all."[45] The focus that Levinas places on the ethical dimension of the relationship between self and other prevents me from reducing those from other religious traditions to a means of gaining knowledge about that religion or using our interactions in order to establish my own religious views as superior.

While the other-focused emphasis of this perspective is admirable, it's significantly limited. The asymmetry of sacrificing myself entirely for the sake of the other doesn't create space for ongoing friendship and interaction between myself and the other where I may also meaningfully express my own views. While affirmation promotes a deep understanding of the other, it doesn't foster mutual understanding. Knitter describes interreligious friendships as "a beautiful, paradoxical blending of differences and commonalities. Friends recognize and affirm how genuinely different they are, but they also feel the possibility of connecting with each other despite these differences."[46] This type of friendship, however, requires some degree of reciprocity rather than asymmetry.[47] Although the other needs to have room to speak, there must also be room for the self to speak while the other listens. Additionally, once a mutual understanding exists between myself and another, I'm able to advocate for her in the fight against religious prejudice. The type of ongoing interfaith engagement we support, using Buber's notion of inclusion

and Volf's metaphor of embrace, allows both the self and the other
to share their views openly and honestly, navigating both their similarities and their differences.

> The type of ongoing interfaith engagement we
> support, using Buber's notion of inclusion and Volf's
> metaphor of embrace, allows both the self and
> the other to share their views openly and honestly,
> navigating both their similarities and their differences.

CONCLUSION

There are strengths to the models of tolerance and affirmation. On
the one hand, tolerance respects others' right to believe differently
and, by promoting civic neutrality, it helps bring an end to discrimination and violence. At times tolerance may be all we're capable of
achieving. For example, when significant disagreements exist but
there is little opportunity for ongoing relationship, tolerating each
other's views is certainly better than nothing at all. On the other hand,
affirmation is also important, albeit limited. There are times when
interfaith engagement may need to take an asymmetrical approach,
hospitably allowing more time and space for minority views to be
presented and explored. This is crucial to remember because, as
Omid Safi aptly states, "We share radically different levels of access
to power, wealth, and privilege. . . . And there are fundamental structural inequalities that shape the parameters in which this conversation takes place."[48] At the same time, the ultimate goal is the mutual
understanding and equality called for by the path of inclusion. As Safi
notes, "The question, and ultimate concern, is how do we create level
playing fields—or, to be more precise, level speaking fields."[49]

The path of inclusion can be challenging. We must learn to stretch
ourselves and become willing to listen to and seek to understand

persons who believe differently while at the same time learning to openly and constructively share our own beliefs. And yet we believe this is the path to follow as we seek to love our neighbors well. We must recognize and prepare for the reality that agreement is impossible on some issues. But, despite this challenge, we can still cooperatively "act on the basis of relative and partial agreements."[50] In order to engage our religious neighbors well, we must cultivate several intellectual and moral virtues that will be explored in the next chapter.

TALK ABOUT IT

+ Where have you seen the models of tolerance and affirmation used to address a conflict? What benefits resulted? What were the limitations? What would have been different had an inclusive approach been taken in those situations?

+ Why is mutuality important for healthy interfaith engagement?

+ Can you imagine a scenario where tolerance or affirmation might be the best outcome for that limited encounter?

GIVE IT A TRY

Chapter seven contains many practical ideas for implementing the ideas in this book. Use the case study approach featured on pages 144-46 as a way to practice applying the model of inclusion to different situations. Discuss how the resolution of the case study might look different if the goal is tolerance or affirmation instead of inclusion.

BEARING WITNESS TO THE LOVE OF JESUS

Rachael McNeal, Interfaith Center coordinator, University of North Florida, and IFYC alum

In interfaith contexts there is a commonly accepted guideline—no proselytizing. Understandably, this is often a turnoff for evangelicals. Evangelism—a Christian practice in which we attempt to "save" people through a relationship with Jesus Christ—is central to evangelical Christianity. With evangelism off limits, evangelicals may feel like they have to water down their faith in order to participate in interfaith work, thus creating a situation in which they do not feel like their most authentic selves.

In my three years of full-time interfaith work I have never once proselytized, yet never in my life have I felt more like I am truly bearing witness to the love of Jesus. I think it is important to remember that evangelism doesn't always look like an explicit attempt to convert others. The role of the Holy Spirit is key in the conversion process of believers—and so sometimes all we really have to do is live in a way that exemplifies and embodies the kingdom. We Christians are often an insular breed, and this is a problem because it means we rarely give ourselves the opportunity to engage authentically and wholly with people of other faiths (or nonfaith). This is why interfaith work is so important for us as Christians; it gives us the opportunity to be the face of God's love to those outside our Christian community.

Interfaith work is important for us as Christians; it gives us the opportunity to be the face of God's love to those outside our Christian community.

I had enriching interfaith friendships prior to working full time in interfaith cooperation, but the interfaith relationships I've built with students are the most dear to me.

I first met Charles, a dedicated secular humanist, at a "coffee and conversation" gathering—a biweekly Interfaith Center event in which a student spends twenty minutes or so speaking about his or her religious or nonreligious identity followed by a question-and-answer session and interfaith dialogue. The speaker that day was a Muslim engineering student. Charles asked her earnest questions rooted in curiosity and an evident desire to better understand others.

I learned from Charles that one can be a principled atheist. In other words, Charles's lack of belief in God was not because he lacked faith but because he had thoughtfully considered the possibility of God and come out deciding he ardently believed there was no God. Charles also decided that, despite all the ugliness in the world, he believed in the good of human nature and in the power of people to make the world better. Even further—he believed that people were obligated to try to make it better.

Through building a relationship with Charles I came to see that one religious group in particular he struggled with was evangelical Christians. Many of his past experiences with Christians had been off-putting, even tense. Evangelism often seemed to him like a tool to put others down and make claims of personal superiority. I had the opportunity to explain that, in fact, most evangelicals want others to know Jesus not because they're egomaniacs (though I'm sure some of us are) but because the idea of someone we care about spending an eternity in hell is more than we can stand.

Charles later told me that through his relationship with me, he was able to view Christianity in a new light. There is a lot Charles and I disagree on—abortion, the existence of God, how the world was created—but we both love to listen to the stories of others. We both are passionate about enriching the lives of others. We both care about the planet. In many ways our differences make our similarities that much more precious.

During my time as the interfaith coordinator at the University of North Florida, I have eaten on the floor with Sikhs at their Gurudwara. I have observed Jummu'ah at the local mosque, attended the celebration of Baha'u'llah's birthday at the Baha'i temple, attended Diwali at the Hindu temple, and walked a labyrinth with pagans. I've worn a turban and a hijab and have been covered head to toe in dyed cornstarch for the spring Hindu festival of Holi. I have done all of these things in the name of listening. Jesus says to love others as you love yourself.

I feel the most loved when I'm being listened to, especially if I'm given an opportunity to share that which is most dear to me—my precious Jesus. In light of this, I constantly set out to allow others to share that which is most dear to them—their faith, their practices, their houses of worship, their celebrations. What a beautiful way to be in relationship. I cannot think of any practice more Christlike than simply being in relationship with another person and I cannot think of a better way to bear witness to the love we know in Jesus than to love others.

> **I feel the most loved when I'm being listened to, especially if I'm given an opportunity to share that which is most dear to me—my precious Jesus. In light of this, I constantly set out to allow others to share that which is most dear to them—their faith, their practices, their houses of worship, their celebrations. What a beautiful way to be in relationship.**

A famous quote by St. Francis is "Always preach the gospel; when necessary use words." But our actions will "preach" only to other Christians if we remain in our insular Christian communities.

5

Cultivating Virtues
for Interfaith Engagement

Some people of faith who might applaud many goals of interfaith dialogue are still concerned about what might be lost in the process. Afraid that dialogue will water down or even erase the significant differences among religions, some religiously committed people choose not to participate.[1] Yet dialogue is an important tool in increasing interfaith understanding and averting conflict. For this reason college campuses need to be places where such productive conversation is fostered and where all students, faculty, and staff can learn to talk, listen, and work with religious others in preparation for participation in a pluralistic society. Ultimately we need to develop qualities that make us well-suited for such participation. In this chapter we focus on three virtues that are essential for effective interfaith engagement: receptive humility, reflective commitment, and imaginative empathy.[2]

There are many ways to approach the topic of virtue within the context of religious diversity. Our thinking has been influenced primarily by the work of Catherine Cornille and Martha Nussbaum. In *The Im-Possibility of Interreligious Dialogue*, Cornille explores five conditions needed for any constructive dialogue—included in these conditions are humility, empathy, and commitment. Two things in particular make Cornille's exploration fruitful. First, her discussion of each "condition" is spacious, helping to illustrate the range of ways in which that particular condition might be realized, varying according to the participants and the purposes of the dialogue. By making room for differing degrees of each condition for dialogue, Cornille's picture enables participants from a range of religious perspectives to find a place at the table. When this happens, each can seek to understand and learn from the other's approach to religious truth while being challenged and stretched in the process.

In addition to Cornille's spacious discussion of each separate condition for dialogue, her placement of conditions side by side enables us to consider how each one relates to the other, sometimes stretching, sometimes suggesting a boundary. Humility or empathy, for example, could make a person feel that she must be open to absolutely anything she might encounter in an interfaith dialogue. But commitment pulls in a different direction, reminding participants that they might spend time "not only informing but also convincing the other of the truth of his or her own beliefs and practices."[3] Each condition also seeks to balance both the sense of solidarity with religious others and the ways in which religions might remain separated from each other.

Martha Nussbaum has written extensively about the interrelated capacities we need to develop if civic life in the diverse society of the United States is to flourish. Her two most relevant books on this subject are *Cultivating Humanity* and *The New Religious Intolerance*.[4] Two emphases in these books are particularly useful here: thinking critically and employing imagination in the development of empathy. We naturally assume we need to apply critical thinking when looking at the beliefs of others, but Nussbaum stresses that we need to be particularly rigorous in scrutinizing our own religious beliefs. Only in this way, says Nussbaum, can we avoid the inconsistency, arrogance, and narcissism that often result when we seek to shield ourselves from criticism.[5] Imaginative empathy (which she also refers to as "sympathetic imagination") is the capacity that enables us to see what the world looks like from a different vantage point.

The qualities and virtues that Cornille and Nussbaum prescribe are interrelated and overlapping—the development of one supports and requires the development of the others. Thus we advocate a combination of qualities that will enable us all to build bridges among different faith communities in order to promote the common good—the civic imperative that we discussed in chapter one. Guided interfaith engagement is crucial in order to foster shared understanding and social and political solidarity. But understanding and solidarity don't just happen overnight: They require active partnership and a refusal to reduce all beliefs to the lowest common denominator.

RECEPTIVE HUMILITY

Receptive humility is crucial if we hope to avoid the bias and hypocrisy often present in religious dialogue. As Nussbaum explains, too often religious persons fail to heed Jesus' question in Matthew 7:3: "And why worry about a speck in your friend's eye when you have a log in your own?" Interaction with persons who believe differently is healthier and more constructive when we're all willing, in humility, to acknowledge the limitations of our own religious views and our need to learn from others.

Humility functions as an antidote to bias and misunderstanding when it's open, "a curious, questioning, and receptive demeanor that says, in effect, 'Here is another human being. I wonder what he (or she) is seeing and feeling right now.'"[6] This receptive aspect of humility is rooted in a desire to seek and receive truth, whether that comes in the form of learning more about why I believe what I believe, coming to recognize the limitations of my own perspectives, or deepening my understanding of those who are different from me. Receptivity may lead me to change my own views and assumptions. Humility helps ensure that dialogue will be, in Rabbi Amy Eilberg's words, "less of a duel and more of a collaboration to find truths and solutions that are life-enhancing for all partners to the conversation."[7]

Many evangelical Christians aren't comfortable submitting their beliefs to such a degree of scrutiny—in fact, some are troubled when their fellow dialogue participants or facilitators ask them to do this. But even these Christians, unwilling to practice what Cornille refers to as "doctrinal humility," can still pursue receptive humility by being "open to constant correction" while seeking to understand what dialogue partners are saying.[8]

For some participants, simply beginning to notice similar practices, shared values, and common goals between people from different faith traditions is real progress and can be a productive starting point. Even if interfaith discussions don't go much beyond this level—which may at times feel superficial—there still exists, says Niebuhr, "the possibility of someone hearing something for the first time, . . . something they come to consider of real value, to explore and build on."[9] This may be a piece of relatively basic information about another religion; it may be the recognition that religious others can share one's own spiritual concerns or find similar practices edifying. Yet each of these realizations helps cultivate receptive humility.

Receptive humility can be developed through interfaith dialogue when such encounters provide the opportunity to reconsider one's own beliefs in a more objective way, viewed through the vantage point of another. This can be difficult and challenging, but it's important. "By gaining exposure to a variety of foreign and conflicting worldviews," wrote one of our students, "we are forced to consider other religious traditions and reexamine our own faiths. Even though some discussions can feel uncomfortable or even threatening, it is that very feeling of discomfort that leads us to truly discover the reasons behind our beliefs."[10] Receptive humility grows as we continue to ask questions and desire to know more. This goes on to fuel the pursuit of ongoing interfaith engagement.

One of the biggest challenges to cultivating humility, however, can arise for those convinced of the "absolute and final truth" of their own religion. They may find themselves listening for flaws in what their dialogue partners are saying, mentally preparing ways to show the superiority of their own beliefs.[11] The preconceptions about their own faith and that of others make it difficult for them to listen receptively and see the many parallels among their own beliefs and those of others. For such a person, simply becoming aware of the tendency to find fault in others' religious beliefs is itself the beginning of humility. As Eilberg says, "When we live out of humility, we can lay claim to that which is rightfully ours, including speaking up for our own views, but we are careful not to deny the other's right to his or hers."[12]

> **When we live out of humility, we can lay claim to that which is rightfully ours, including speaking up for our own views, but we are careful not to deny the other's right to his or hers.**
>
> AMY EILBERG

REFLECTIVE COMMITMENT

While receptive humility is a crucial condition for constructive dialogue, it's not sufficient. Healthy interfaith engagement should also provide opportunities for participants to sincerely express their religious beliefs and commitments. Cornille argues that if participants

didn't come to the table connected to a religious tradition, the dialogue might be interesting and valuable but it wouldn't be interreligious. Commitment to one's religious tradition provides both "a
solid point of departure and a critical place of return."[13] How does
commitment relate to dialogue? Cornille says authentic dialogue
"contains a missionary and apologetic dimension."[14] This is the case,
she continues, because religious identity includes seeing one's own
beliefs and practices as worthy of commitment, "as the lens through
which the world is understood and evaluated."[15] So it should come
as no surprise when an evangelical student of ours, having sought
to convince others in his interfaith dialogue group of the truth of
Christianity, mused, "The way I understand it is that they should
feel honored that I would be willing to share the truth with them
rather than not share out of fear of offending them."[16]

There's an obvious challenge here for interfaith engagement:
We must learn to balance our commitments and convictions with
receptive humility. In our dialogues and our reflections together,
we need to ask how we might affirm both the virtues of open-
mindedness and of faithfulness to a tradition.[17] Those who find
openness to be a natural approach to religious difference may need
to cultivate respect for those who desire to convert others to their
own commitments. Those who possess a strong commitment to their
own tradition, on the other hand, may need to be reassured that a
person can listen, seek to understand, and even appreciate aspects of
another religion without compromising commitment to one's own.
In our interactions with our religious neighbors, we need to learn
when to leave some issues off the table, when to listen, when to speak,
and when to focus on common ground rather than differences.[18]

All who participate in interfaith dialogue can strive together to
develop the sort of reflective commitment that includes the ability to
"think deeply and critically about fundamental questions in general,
as well as about [one's] own fundamental beliefs, attachments,

and presuppositions."[19] Reflective commitment is evident in those who are aware both of the reasons they remain committed to their beliefs and the reasonable grounds for doubting them. It can be seen in those who are willing to entertain tough questions without abandoning the beliefs that one is "still investigating or allowing others to question."[20] One of our students, reflecting on things he'd learned through interfaith dialogue, made a similar point when he observed, "If we fail to genuinely listen to others for fear of being spiritually challenged, we cannot hope to gain greater intimacy with God."[21] Another student said, "To be truly open is to genuinely consider others' worldviews and alter or augment one's current belief system according to one's sense of reason. It is not closed-minded to disagree with other religious traditions, nor is it heretical to agree with components of foreign faiths."[22] Both of these student comments provide glimpses of reflective commitment.

For commitment to be truly reflective, we must be willing to engage in what Nussbaum refers to as "Socratic scrutiny" or "rigorous critical thinking." Socratic scrutiny involves an ongoing "critical examination of oneself and one's traditions," seeking to live what Socrates called "the examined life."[23] Scrutiny of our own beliefs doesn't mean we have to avoid critiquing other religions and simply ignore the significant differences between them, though. Rather, it involves developing a more reflective understanding of one's own position in light of an increasingly more accurate understanding of another's position.

In finding a balance between humility and commitment, we come to recognize that it's possible to admire an aspect of another religious tradition without weakening our commitment to our own. In fact, what I value in another tradition may actually help to strengthen my own religious practice. Our students have had the opportunity to experience this. Several have admiringly noted the commitment displayed by Jews and Muslims they have met in interfaith dialogues, observing that Christians could certainly learn from such devotion. One student, having been impressed by the commitment and passion expressed by an imam he met at an interfaith dialogue, concluded that "Muslims take their stance on religious issues a lot more seriously than many Christians today."[24]

IMAGINATIVE EMPATHY

Both Cornille and Nussbaum recognize that empathy is a cognitive as well as a moral virtue. It involves a desire to learn intellectually about another religion and its adherents as well as "a willingness and ability to penetrate into the religious mindset of the other and understand him or her from within."[25] For this to occur, says Cornille, one must have sympathy for the religious other—which includes "personal warmth and affection toward the other person" but also openness to the "meaningfulness and worth of his or her religious life. It includes respect for and interest in the beliefs and practices of the other."[26] Empathy involves humanizing the other, seeking to get to know members of other religious communities in direct and personal ways. At minimum, such recognition helps us come to see those who follow other faiths as "real people . . . [who] earnestly believe," as one of our students reflected.[27] In this way the religious other becomes more than an abstract representation of a particular tradition and becomes my religious neighbor.

Some of our students, particularly those who have participated in off-campus interfaith dialogues and have subsequently developed relationships with those they met, go beyond this recognition and begin challenging their own beliefs. One student asked this question: "What about those other people—the professors, and imams, and rabbis—intellectual, deep people, who seem to believe sincerely what they are saying? What if they are right?"[28]

A person seeking to reflect seriously on such a question may have to exercise imagination in order to consider what the other's beliefs and practices mean, what they look like from the inside. This sort of imaginative empathy includes "the ability to think what it might be like to be in the shoes of a person different from oneself, to be an intelligent reader of that person's story, and to understand the emotions and desires that someone so placed might have."[29] In cultivating such an imagination, we're starting to understand difference from a new vantage point. This in turn helps us realize on a deep level that our neighbors are not "forbiddingly alien and other" but that we share "many problems and possibilities."[30]

Those who come to see admirable qualities in the beliefs and practices of others often articulate part of what Cornille refers to as "interconnection." Simply put, interconnection is "a sense of commonality or solidarity among religions, and of the relevance of the other religion for one's own religious tradition."[31] Interconnection might mean sharing common concerns over issues such as environmental destruction, justice for the poor, and the role of religion in civil society. It also might mean identifying "universal features" of various religions, including "a sense of being in a life that transcends this world's selfish little interests, a commitment to self-surrender, freedom, and loving and harmonious affections."[32] One of our students described this sense of interconnection when he said that "other religious traditions also promote the importance of family values, and many religions, especially the three religions stemming from Abraham, share near identical moral codes."[33] Developing a sense of interconnection across faith traditions helps contribute to our feelings of empathy toward our religious neighbors.

Some Christians are surprised by when empathy is easiest—and hardest—to cultivate. Most of our students expect to find compatriots in their fellow Christian interfaith dialogue participants, assuming common theological commitments and concerns. Instead, they frequently notice, as Robert Nash and DeMethra Bradley observe, that "there is as much spiritual difference within most particular religious narratives or traditions as there is between and among different religious groups."[34] One of our students found that remarks made by fellow Christians "sharply conflicted with [his] own beliefs, even more so than the speakers of other religions."[35] Even further, he commented that he respected a Muslim speaker the most, admiring this man because he was "the one who was most unafraid to present his own beliefs. . . . He did not need to back up his point with pluralistic views, which I greatly appreciated."[36]

This student's admiration of the Muslim speaker's firm belief helped him begin to recognize the interconnection that might be the start of imaginative empathy for this religious neighbor. Imaginative empathy doesn't require agreement with or endorsement of the views held by another person. But it does help us see and feel the depth of others' commitments, to "learn that other worlds of thought and feeling exist."[37]

Nussbaum places three important conditions on imaginative capacity that aim to protect against misuse or misappropriation of this crucial skill. First, imaginative empathy must be rooted in an ethical commitment to do no harm. This means that I genuinely have concern and sympathy for the other as a fellow human being. At the same time, however, I don't have to accept or endorse any religious practices that violate the rights of others or that harm others.[38] Critique is at times necessary, but critique must always be informed. This leads to Nussbaum's second condition: Imaginative empathy must be rooted in factual truth. We must be sure we attempt to genuinely and accurately understand the other's views before we criticize them. Third, Nussbaum emphasizes that the purpose of imaginative empathy is crucial. We shouldn't use this capacity to manipulate others. For example, I fail to show empathy if my singular motive for building a relationship with a person of a different faith is to convert this person.[39]

When we cultivate imaginative empathy, we reach a central goal of interfaith interaction—balancing receptive humility and reflective commitment. We learn to think and speak respectfully about various ways of life through taking time to listen and empathize, entering imaginatively into another person's story. But this never requires a "hands-off attitude to criticism of what one encounters."[40] This balance between openness and honesty, between a willingness to change and a desire to remain true to one's commitments, is articulated well by one of the participants in "The Faith Club," an interfaith discussion and support group described in a book by the same name. Speaking of the impact of her years of involvement in this group, this participant said, "I still speak as a Jew, but [as] a Jew with a Palestinian friend."[41]

VIRTUES FOR THE COMMON GOOD

A common theme shared by all systems of virtue ethics is a commitment to bridge the personal with the social. This means that cultivating virtues is never merely about becoming a good person. Rather, the end goal of becoming virtuous always points beyond the self toward a better form of life together. In order to address the civic concerns outlined in the first chapter of this book, we must think beyond ourselves to the essential role that receptive humility, reflective commitment, and imaginative empathy can play in developing friendships and, ultimately, in cultivating peace.

According to Eilberg, the fundamental work of peace-building is for us to "move beyond generalized thinking about 'the other'" and instead "see the other as a trustworthy and admirable human being, even in the presence of real religious and/or ideological differences."[42] The virtues needed for, and deepened by, interfaith engagement do just that. Receptive humility invites the other into my intellectual and moral space, reflective commitment motivates my continued investment in working with others for the common good, and imaginative empathy bolsters my belief and hope in the possibility of peace. As I engage with those who believe differently, I practice using what Eck calls "bridging speech," which is the ability to communicate across faith lines—a skill needed for effective common action.

The virtues of receptive humility, reflective commitment, and imaginative empathy can start to be learned through books and films. But it's in the context of face-to-face encounters and budding relationships with real religious others that such qualities can mature.[43] In our work with evangelical Christians, we've seen these encounters to be energizing, motivating them to deeper spiritual commitment, to acts of service, and possibly also to cultivate relationships across faith lines. Others may find themselves frustrated when they can't understand another—or when they can't get another to understand them. Some may be deeply unsettled, not sure what to do with the questions that interfaith conversations raise. In each case we can work to provide the necessary challenge and support as we all learn to relate to each other amid our differences.

While we're convinced that Christians need to move beyond our own religious bubbles, we also recognize that these bubbles can be helpful spaces for cultivating the virtues and skills needed in building constructive relationships with persons of different faiths. How we can go about using our faith-based college campuses and organizations to meet this goal is the focus of the next two chapters.

TALK ABOUT IT

• Why is it important to balance receptive humility and reflective commitment? What might happen if we fail to cultivate one or the other?

- In your own experience, when has empathy been easiest and hardest to cultivate and express? Why do you think this was the case?

- What is the end goal of cultivating these virtues? How might these virtues positively impact your surrounding community and world?

GIVE IT A TRY

Chapter seven contains many practical ideas for implementing the ideas in this book. Play the doubting-believing game described on pages 136-39 to practice receptive humility, reflective commitment, and imaginative empathy. You might decide to use faith as a topic for the game, or you might choose to discuss a current political debate or controversial issue facing your campus or community.

CULTIVATING A DEEPER UNDERSTANDING OF THE DIVERSE COMMUNITIES OF WHICH I AM A PART

Anna Wilson, program coordinator for the CollegePoint Initiative, College Possible, and Bethel University alum

As an undergraduate I was offered the opportunity to work with Marion Larson as a student researcher on a project focused on interfaith engagement. Little did I know that this work would become a hallmark of my undergraduate education. Interfaith engagement has cultivated a deeper understanding of myself and the diverse communities of which I am a part. This understanding has been crucial to my success after college as a person of faith, both in moving abroad with a Fulbright scholarship and in working with low-income, high-achieving students through a college access organization.

As we began working on this project, Dr. Larson asked me why I thought interfaith dialogues were important. This was 2009 and even though it was eight years after the 9/11 attacks, I had gone to high school and was nearing my completion of college in a world that was very wary of Muslims. When I was asked this question, my first thought was to convey the importance of figuring out how to live among people of other religions—especially religions that made us afraid. Not knowing how to articulate this nuance, I ungracefully said that "racism isn't really an issue anymore, but problems of religious diversity are definitely very divisive."

Ultimately, it would be through studying religious diversity that I would be able to understand racial diversity, but it took me a few years to understand the ignorance of that particular statement I had uttered in Dr. Larson's office. I was raised in one of the most racially diverse communities in Minnesota; it was also a highly segregated community, a reality that I grew up blind to. I then attended a primarily white, upper-middle-class Christian university. Even as an open-minded and compassionate person, I did not yet have the tools to understand systems of injustice that underrepresented people face. I had been taught that it was important to care for people who were less fortunate and to love others, but I was afraid to engage in conversations around race, let alone racism. It was easier for me to think that racism didn't exist than to talk about it.

I wasn't afraid, however, to talk about religious diversity. To discuss, read, research, and participate in interfaith dialogues offered a thoughtful framework for me to engage with difference. I was interested, curious, and open to people who were different from me, but I hadn't ever had the opportunity to intentionally engage with diversity—religious, racial, cultural, or otherwise. Interfaith engagement taught me the virtues necessary to mindfully and meaningfully interact with an "other." On the most basic level, I learned the nuts and bolts of what people of other religious backgrounds believed. I also learned that Jews, Muslims, and Christians are all connected through Abraham and that people I had thought were so very different from me were actually quite similar. Furthermore, the people I met actually felt familiar. Sitting at a table with people from the Jewish and Muslim faiths, I was reminded of people from my childhood church or my home community. They felt like the grandfathers, aunts, cousins, and family friends I had grown up having conversations with around my family's dinner table.

Hearing a Muslim man defend the words of the Qur'an and a Jewish woman explain how she interpreted the Torah sounded like conversations I regularly heard among Christian peers in my college classes. I began to see that it wasn't just about one's religious beliefs but about how one holds them. I began to question how I held my own faith. While it was challenging at times, interfaith engagement showed me what it might look like to hold my faith openly and with complexity. Moreover, I learned that in order to engage fruitfully in discussion, I couldn't simply abandon what I believed. In fact, I had to seriously evaluate my beliefs.

After learning a great deal about how to engage religious diversity, I graduated from my faith-based community at Bethel University and moved to Kosice, Slovakia, with a Fulbright scholarship. While in Kosice, I was the only American teaching at a French-bilingual high school with a mixed faculty of French and Slovak teachers. Most students and faculty had very negative ideas of what being an American teacher meant, ideas that were loaded with American stereotypes and also assumed "Christian missionary" stereotypes. I knew I would have challenges building trust within my new culturally diverse community. Fortunately, I already had practice building trust among people from different backgrounds from the interfaith dialogues I had participated in while in college.

While teaching at the high school and living in Kosice, I felt tempted to shed my American and Christian identities because it felt so much easier to assimilate. I felt the same tension I had felt in college: do I fully embrace my American identity or do I abandon it completely? Mostly I had to learn to embrace the complexity. I had to learn to hold my identity while also embracing others, to allow myself to change when I needed to, and to allow parts of my identity to remain misunderstood or different. Although it was difficult, my previous participation in interfaith dialogues had given me tools that helped me think well about my experience. I was able to change when I needed to, listen to others, ask good questions, and let go of my defenses. This allowed me to thrive in my new community.

> My previous participation in interfaith dialogues had given me tools that helped me think well about my experience. I was able to change when I needed to, listen to others, ask good questions, and let go of my defenses. This allowed me to thrive in my new community.

From practicing interfaith dialogues at home to navigating intercultural relationships abroad, I thought I had rich experiences with diversity. And with these experiences under my belt I thought I was prepared for my new job—working with a college access organization called College Possible. My job was to partner with students from a wide array of backgrounds as they began their journey toward college.

I began working at a very diverse high school during a time when racial tensions heightened in our country with news coverage of Trayvon Martin, Ferguson, Missouri, and countless police shootings of unarmed black men. Seeing the tragedies that my students faced while also understanding the systems of injustice that perpetuated their tragedies was remarkably humbling. For the first time I was able to critically examine my own identity as a middle-class white Christian woman, how my privilege impacted my work with students, and how I unintentionally participated in injustice. While these were hard questions to grapple with, they were important for me to understand in order to be the kind of support my students needed. My ability to recognize my identity allowed me to engage fully with my students without fear, defense, or condescension.

Interfaith engagement has been absolutely imperative in my learning to navigate the complexities of diversity in our society and in our world. Because of my experience, I believe that knowing how to work with people who are different should be emphasized on college campuses, particularly on faith-based campuses where religious diversity is often minimal.

Our world requires us to engage with people who are different from us. It is increasingly "normal" to work with and live among people from the Muslim, Jewish, or Buddhist faiths, or (increasingly) no faith at all. Growing tensions around immigration, race, and gender identity are forcing hard conversations and even legislative changes. My experiences with interfaith engagement taught me to view these changes with hopefulness and showed me how to engage with our diverse world with grace, curiosity, and courage.

6

Inside the Bubble

CREATING A NURTURING LEARNING ENVIRONMENT

Thus far we've spent several chapters discussing the importance of preparing to lovingly engage a religiously diverse world. We've explored what loving our religious neighbors should look like and identified the traits we need to develop to do that well. We've also discussed the concern that some Christians may feel at the prospect of interfaith interaction, fearing a possible loss of Christian identity and compromised commitment. We recognize that some notions of identity and some commitments will be challenged through interaction with religious others, but we believe that such challenge can produce good results. As the parables of the lost son and the good Samaritan remind us, we need to reexamine many of our thoughts about our religious neighbors, recognizing that we have much to learn from each other.

Many questions are likely to arise as we go beyond simply learning a few facts about religions other than Christianity and instead seek to get to know and learn from our religious neighbors. Becoming comfortable with questions is a crucial step toward learning to love one's neighbors well. In order to do this, we can utilize what many refer to as "bubble" spaces, whether that's an exclusively Christian campus or classroom or an organization that exists to help Christians mature in their faith. Within these "bubbles" we have the opportunity to create spaces of trust where it's safe to process what we're learning, both before and after we interact with those who believe differently. In addition, intrafaith discussions within the bubble help make evident that we don't have to step outside these spheres of similarity in order to encounter difficult disagreements and differences. Bubble spaces aren't as homogenous and conflict-free as we might initially imagine.

In this chapter we'll explore in more detail the idea that encountering challenging ideas and questions can actually help strengthen faith commitments and offer some advice for cultivating healthy environments in which to process challenging ideas.

DEVELOPING WORLDVIEW COMMITMENT AND AN ECUMENICAL ORIENTATION

Theorists and researchers who address moral and spiritual development concur that the college years are a critically important time to "reexamine . . . and to reassemble a personally constructed, critically examined, deeper faith that grows as the intellectual life of the student is also maturing."[1] Recognizing this, a goal often articulated by those who work with Christian college students is for them to come to exhibit a "maturing faith," a central feature of which is the student's "genuine ownership" of her faith.[2] One helpful definition of "ownership" comes from the research team working with the Collegiate Religious and Spiritual Climate Survey (CRSCS), a large-scale project examining what they refer to as "worldview commitment," defined as the extent to which those studied "(1) are committed to their worldview, (2) feel their worldview gives their life meaning, and (3) have put a lot of thought into the beliefs they hold."[3]

Thoughtful commitment to a worldview that's personally meaningful—this certainly sounds like an important part of what education hopes to accomplish and what we as people of faith seek to develop in ourselves. But reflective commitment (as we called it in chapter five) by itself isn't adequate, because it doesn't say anything about the way a person with such commitment will treat others—particularly others whose beliefs differ from her own. Such commitment (and its expression) ought also to be shaped by the other two qualities discussed in chapter five—receptive humility and imaginative empathy. These two qualities have much in common with what Alyssa Rockenbach and Matthew Mayhew refer to as an "ecumenical orientation." Those with this orientation "have an interest in learning about diverse religious perspectives, believe that core values underlie and connect diverse religious traditions, and accept people with worldviews that differ from their own."[4]

Openness to pluralism and diversity have long been part of various developmental frameworks that inform the mindset and practice of many in higher education, note Rockenbach and Mayhew. Three such frameworks they reference are those developed by Arthur Chickering and Linda Reisser, Larry Braskamp, and Sharon Daloz Parks. Chickering and Reisser's model includes developing mature interpersonal relationships, a maturity which "necessitates challenging one's (perhaps inaccurate) assumptions and learning to value cultural differences."[5] In his developmental model, Braskamp speaks of the significance of global citizenship, which he describes as "the degree to which students are understanding of, open to, and appreciative of cultural differences."[6] Similarly, in her discussion of faith development, Parks sees "openness to others" as an important step in the move toward mature adult faith.[7] These developmental theorists all sound potentially consistent with the Christian goal of seeking to become "whole and holy people" who can serve Christ and the world as global citizens. If we wish to accomplish such a goal, we ought to seek to cultivate both an ecumenical orientation and worldview commitment through guided interfaith engagement.

How Can Worldview Commitment and Ecumenical Orientation Go Together?

Not all people of faith fully support the development of an ecumenical orientation. For them, worldview commitment is centrally important and must be protected. These believers, observes Robert Nash, are convinced that they possesses "an absolute, revealed truth . . . that is unimpeachable, immutable, and final." They understand their responsibility as one of "deliver[ing] this Truth to others as an act of love and generosity."[8] For such believers, development of an ecumenical orientation—and a regular demonstration of religious tolerance—"can be understood as a lack of religious conviction or, worse, hypocrisy."[9] Wanting to avoid hypocrisy and retain their strong commitment, these believers often avoid interfaith dialogues or approach such events skeptically. When they do participate, they often find that an ecumenical orientation and a religiously pluralistic mindset are the default perspectives, with religious exclusivism seen as judgmental and arrogant.[10] Hearing such messages simply affirms the false impression that worldview commitment and ecumenical orientation are incompatible.

It's certainly possible for those who believe their religion to be the only path to God to communicate this conviction in ways that sound judgmental and arrogant. But this isn't a necessary result of religious exclusivism. Charles Soukup and James Keaten helpfully point out that the issue in interfaith interactions isn't that of "pluralist" versus "exclusivist." Instead, the issue is whether a person responds to religious otherness in a "dehumanizing" or in a "humanizing" way.[11] In fact, they note, it's possible for both pluralists and exclusivists to be dehumanizing toward those with whom they disagree: Dehumanizing pluralists see those who "do not embrace pluralism as 'closed-minded' and 'self-important'"; similarly, dehumanizing exclusivists interpret religious difference as "threatening and potentially dangerous."[12] By contrast, "anyone with a humanizing response, regardless of their orientation toward religious otherness, is capable of engaging in productive encounters across faiths."[13] Particularly for Christians who believe that Christ's claims are unique and that trust in him is central to salvation, it's important to hear that there can be room at the interfaith dialogue table for religious exclusivists. Sociologist of religion Robert Wuthnow concurs: "Respect must also extend to those who wish, in a spirit of goodwill and without reliance on coercion or legislation, to share their ideas in hopes of persuading others to join their faith."[14]

Religious exclusivists can ensure that they aren't dehumanizing in their response to religious neighbors by holding their worldview commitments in productive tension with an ecumenical orientation. An ecumenical orientation requires the virtue of receptive humility, in which we recognize that our sinfulness and our human limitations will

The issue is whether a person responds to religious otherness in a "dehumanizing" or in a "humanizing" way.

at times lead us to reach incorrect conclusions and make erroneous claims about the truth.[15] Humility also prevents us from too quickly assuming that the beliefs of our dialogue partners are false.[16] And we seek in humility to cultivate a receptive spirit, because we recognize that "signs of divine truth may show up in surprising places— such as in other religions."[17] Thus, humility enables religious exclusivists to remain simultaneously open to other traditions and committed to their own.[18] Mikael Stenmark calls this perspective "tentative" exclusivism, a mindset particularly consistent with the virtues of receptive humility and reflective commitment that we discussed in chapter five.[19]

Healthy interaction with persons of other faiths is really a matter of learning to "draw the line between conviction and intolerance," says Wuthnow. But this requires each of us to think about what we believe and how we ought to interact with each other amid incommensurate claims about religious truth.[20] Thus, imaginative empathy should also be an important component of religious exclusivism. By cultivating the capacity to see the world from the other's perspective, we become aware of the strength of commitment, and perhaps even exclusivism, of the other's religious beliefs. Through imaginative empathy we can affirm both the virtues of open-mindedness and faithfulness—that is, of ecumenical orientation and of worldview commitment.

Interfaith engagement helps to make this real. For example, we once took a group of Christian students to an interfaith engagement event at a local mosque. Although the event was supposed to be a chance to discuss how our respective religions prompted us to participate in community service, it ended up being a presentation on the superiority of Islam over Christianity. Rather than finding their faith shaken by the event, however, our students came away still committed to their own beliefs and also more receptive toward Muslim believers. They came to see that evangelical Christians aren't the only ones convinced that they possess the truth about God. Nor are evangelicals the only ones who identify substantial theological problems or limitations in another's religion. Becoming aware of their similar stance toward faith helped our students develop imaginative empathy toward these Muslim neighbors.

Cultivating a Healthy Bubble

To make such an outcome possible, we and our students needed to be able to admit that learning can be scary, particularly when we encounter ideas and perspectives that challenge our usual ways of seeing. What's needed is a supportive space in which trust can be fostered—the kind of trust that makes difficult learning possible, the kind of trust that helps to "lubricate the inevitable frictions of social life."[21] Fostering trust is a multidimensional process. It involves the attributes displayed by the teacher or facilitator, the creation of a hospitable learning environment, and lowering the risk threshold for participants. This is where "bubbles" can be particularly valuable: They can be places where we deepen our own faith commitments while also developing and practicing skills we can then use in building bridges with our religious neighbors.

Building trust. One way to think about fostering trust between facilitators and participants is to return to the model of inclusion developed in chapter four. In advocating openness toward each other and toward the ideas we explore together, we again must refrain from the extremes of tolerance and affirmation. We shouldn't merely tolerate the ideas expressed by those in our classrooms or groups, nor take a stance of neutrality toward them, because this fails to cultivate the healthy relationships needed for the safe and courageous exploration of difficult ideas. Similarly, affirming all ideas and questions raised in discussion without close reflection on what's being expressed doesn't do much to promote intellectual, spiritual, and personal growth.[22] Instead, we must build the trusting relationships needed for an inclusive space where genuine learning can take place.

Inclusion seeks to hold some features of both tolerance and affirmation in tension. For this reason, it's fair to say that "the educational situation requires the striking of a delicate balance between dedication and detachment, between intimacy and distance."[23] And this can occur only through encounters that acknowledge the particularity of each person and context—seeking to explore together the various implications of individual perspectives and of various traditions.[24] Such encounters are fostered in spaces where everyone feels that they're taken seriously—a necessary precondition if trust is to develop, thereby making risk-taking and deep learning possible.[25]

The trustworthy teacher or leader ought to model the virtues we discussed in chapter five: receptive humility, reflective commitment, and imaginative empathy. The teacher must also be self-aware, not forgetting her desire to help participants grow holistically. Because of such a goal—and recognizing the potential vulnerability of learners in her care—the facilitator must be willing to take responsibility for the influence that she exerts on participants. Rather than seeking to impose her own views, the facilitator seeks to help each participant take his or her own worldview seriously.[26]

Learners view humble, authentic, and appropriately self-revealing teachers or facilitators as trustworthy. Stephen Brookfield and Mary Hess suggest that personal trustworthiness includes "demonstrating the ways we [ourselves] are in constant formation, particularly how we are continually forced to question and rethink beliefs and actions with which we have grown comfortable."[27] Leaders should be "willing and eager to engage in the same kind of . . . reflection" that they ask of their participants.[28]

In order to cultivate trust, facilitators should also remain open to the ideas shared by participants, modeling the same sort of hospitality that we seek to show our religious neighbors. Regardless of a participant's particular perspective on various issues, a trustworthy facilitator demonstrates a willingness to take each person's search for meaning seriously, recognizing the significant role that sacred texts and other spiritual authorities play in many people's lives. This includes allowing room for several possible perspectives, seeking to equip participants to "navigate on their own" rather than pushing them to embrace particular views that may be incompatible with their religious or spiritual beliefs.[29] When disagreements arise, as they inevitably will, we can remind each other that agreement isn't the goal—but "charitable comprehension is."[30]

Overall, a trustworthy teacher or facilitator accepts that we're all learners in the process of growing intellectually, socially, and spiritually. None of us has all of the answers; all of us have questions and will make mistakes. So a facilitator must avoid making assumptions about the questions and fears people might bring to a conversation. Instead we should recognize and encourage the possibilities we see in each other. Buber describes the role of teacher or leader this way: "I have been put here and have to accept them as they are—but not as they now are in this moment, no, as they really are, as they can become."[31]

Creating a hospitable environment. Because significant learning can be unsettling, it's crucial for the leader or facilitator to seek to create a classroom environment that's hospitable—one that's welcoming, affirming, and safe. Such a space needs to allow room for feelings to be addressed, encouraging vulnerability and even expressions of anger or doubt, without fear of judgment.[32] Creating a supportive space for the development of worldview commitment and an ecumenical orientation requires the growth of trust between leaders and participants, as well as among participants themselves.

Trust among participants is crucial for cultivating a hospitable learning space because it feels risky to "step out of the safety" of existing perspectives[33]—even if one is only doing so temporarily in order to understand new ideas. Trust is fostered where there's a culture of dialogue and conversation rather than argument and debate. While debates can be engaging, pushing participants to argue for a position can be counterproductive. All too often, when we become uncomfortable, we defensively overemphasize the good of our own position, underemphasize its limitations, and neglect the strengths of the other position altogether.[34]

To avoid this, Nash, Bradley, and Chickering identify three attitudes in particular that participants need to bring to the conversation and work to develop together. Participants should first seek to "open conversational spaces" through practicing what these authors refer to as the "golden rule of moral conversation: listen to others as we would be listened to. We need to question and challenge others as we would be questioned and challenged."[35] Second, each participant needs to be willing to recognize that she isn't the only one in the room with insight, that others also have contributions to make. For this reason, each idea needs to be given at least an initial right to be heard, and each participant works to listen in order to understand—rather than to correct or argue.[36] Finally, particularly when encountering difficult or controversial topics, participants work together to look for what they might have in common. This might involve trying to "embrace . . . even the smallest kernel of truth" in perspectives with which one disagrees— and if that's not possible, at least making a "commitment to try to understand (not agree with)" what's so important about the perspective "of the other for the other."[37]

In other words, if we hope to cultivate an environment for healthy dialogue, we need to learn to practice respect, in the sense of that word's Latin root: to "look back, again and again, to find value in what one might have initially opposed or dismissed."[38] Brookfield and Hess describe respect this way: "When we show respect for others, we work diligently at seeing them clearly . . . , at trying to understand as much as we can the ways they have experienced the world, and the development of their own spirituality."[39] A climate of trust and respect can be supported by leaving plenty of time for reflection and discussion, thus making room to consider "how certain ideas matter" to others and ourselves.[40]

A respectful and hospitable learning space isn't necessarily a "safe" space, though. Many Christians desire a bubble in which their beliefs won't be challenged or questioned, but transformative learning doesn't happen in completely safe and comfortable spaces.[41] Jenny Small's research reinforces this claim when she describes experiences that promote growth as those "characterized by critical self-reflection in the face of constructive, challenging interactions."[42] By contrast, she notes that experiences that "did not promote growth, or even stifled it, were . . . often associated with protecting the status quo within comfortable surroundings."[43]

There are certainly times where being surrounded by like-minded peers is a needed respite from uncomfortable, and even unsettling, encounters with difference. In these cases separate safe spaces (or "bubbles") can help build a common identity, reinforce the worthiness of that identity, and support commitment to that identity. But bubbles don't help us directly address the fear that keeps us from venturing beyond such spaces. If we aren't willing to interact with beliefs and values different from our own, we're unlikely to develop strong faith commitment and learn to love our neighbors well. Instead of conceiving of the bubble merely as a safe space, we should instead seek to utilize it as a supportive space, where we have the opportunity to explore challenging ideas, process uncomfortable experiences, and practice new skills together without fear.

> Instead of conceiving of the bubble merely as a safe space, we should instead seek to utilize it as a supportive space.

Lowering the risk. Stephen Brookfield reminds us that significant challenges and deep emotions can accompany learning, most often when learning involves exploring new perspectives and thinking critically.[44] Students whose learning causes them to question their beliefs may fear "cultural suicide," seeing the change in their thinking as an "act of betrayal" to family, pastor, peers, themselves, or even God.[45] They also may feel anxious when they begin leaving the safety and security of their familiar ways of thinking and acting, wondering how to proceed because they feel they suddenly lack the support they once felt.[46] While such fears won't dissipate readily, facilitators can help allay fear and cultivate trust simply by acknowledging this dynamic.[47]

Addressing fears directly and lowering the perceived risk of interfaith engagement is crucial. The goal isn't to remove discomfort and challenge altogether. In fact, research suggests that experiences that promote growth are most commonly characterized by "critical self-reflection in the face of constructive, challenging interactions."[48] At the same time, however, many people turn away from challenging situations when the discomfort they experience is too strong.[49] This means that effective learning is most likely to happen when there's an appropriate amount of challenge with limited actual risk. According to Small, anxiety increases when students don't feel comfortable speaking openly about their own beliefs, when they perceive competition between religious traditions, and when they fear being judged as less committed or devout than other members of their own religious tradition.[50] Participants need to feel safe to practice, make mistakes, ask questions, and change their minds.

Intrafaith dialogue within the context of a "bubble" can provide a constructive way to address these fears. One benefit of intrafaith dialogue is that it can be a time of what Alan Ray calls "charging the batteries."[51] Conversations with other Christians can help us better understand and interpret the "liturgical, educational, communal, and individual" dimensions of our own religious tradition.[52] Charging the batteries might include giving participants the opportunity to "engage in religious services appropriate to their needs and responsive to their religious calendars."[53] So, for example, Catholic and Lutheran participants may plan activities for the Lenten season, Episcopal participants may choose to utilize the Book of Common Prayer in their activities, and evangelical students may plan a service that features contemporary praise music. Ray also stresses the importance of opening these events so that "alienated or disaffected nominal members" also feel welcome.[54]

Charging the batteries can help build bridges between different Christian groups. It's important to recognize, however, that intrafaith dialogue comes with its own set of challenges. When engaging in these types of conversations, we need to remember that diversity exists even within the bubble. Intrafaith dialogue can be surprising and upsetting for participants who are forced to confront (perhaps for the first time) the diversity within Christianity. Christians come from different sociocultural backgrounds, are divided along many lines (Catholic, mainline Protestants, evangelical Protestants, Pentecostals, orthodox, and fundamentalist, to name only a few), have different liturgical practices, approach Scripture differently, and have differing views of many challenging cultural issues such as gender and sexuality.

Intrafaith dialogue can also be challenging because participants may have anxiety about "being deemed lesser-than members of their own identity groups," and sometimes intrafaith conversations turn into "forms of religious competition that might raise individuals' insecurities."[55] In fact, "disagreements between students from the same group are sometimes more fraught with emotion than those between students from different groups."[56] For these reasons, it's important that intrafaith dialogue also follow the model of inclusion described in chapter four and that participants focus on practicing the virtues outlined in chapter five: humility, commitment, and empathy.

> **When engaging in these types of conversations, we need to remember that diversity exists even within the bubble.**

Not only can intrafaith dialogue foster mutual understanding and harmony amidst differences within a religious bubble; it also creates an opportunity for students to develop and practice transferable skills to use when they leave the bubble to cross the bridge. Skills in conflict resolution and peace-building, for example, are crucial in both contexts. We know we need to learn to interact graciously with our religious neighbors, but we also need to learn to cultivate peace within our own religious communities.[57] So not only does intrafaith engagement help prepare us to encounter religious others; it also helps us learn how to engage each other well.

Developing the skills of inclusion within a bubble cultivates the courage and confidence needed to interact with one's neighbors constructively, both within the bubble and beyond. On our path to loving both God and neighbors well, we need to strike a balance between supporting worldview commitment and cultivating an ecumenical orientation toward those who believe differently. Practical ways to develop both sets of skills will be discussed in the next chapter.

TALK ABOUT IT

- How can a religious exclusivist avoid dehumanizing others? How can a pluralist avoid dehumanizing others?

- What are some of the characteristics of a healthy "bubble"? How could a healthy bubble space develop on your campus or in your community?

- What is the value of intrafaith dialogue? What sort of internal conversations might it be helpful for your community to have?

GIVE IT A TRY

Chapter seven includes many practical ideas. Read about the "community day" exercise on pages 131-36. Then, plan a community day as an alternative to your regular class or meeting routine. You might choose to discuss what you're learning in this book by having participants come with questions or ideas that haven't come up yet in your conversations. (Remember, no new readings or assignments can be planned for this session!)

THERE IS POWER IN STORIES AND FACE-TO-FACE INTERACTION

Amy Poppinga, assistant professor of history, Bethel University

When I decided to leave my job teaching high school to pursue a graduate degree, my goal was to learn more about the religion of Islam so that I could better connect with the increasing number of Muslim students. To be honest, it would be more accurate to say that I wanted to learn how to connect at all, as I had limited ability to relate to and interact with students from diverse religious backgrounds.

This was professionally and personally troubling to me. I had entered teaching believing I was well-prepared academically, that I was adequately equipped with the skills necessary to succeed, and that my enthusiasm and commitment to student success would compensate for my lack of experience. Well, no one had prepared me to engage religious difference, not only as a necessary part of being a history teacher, but more importantly, as a necessary part of being a committed Christian in a diverse and pluralistic society. However, it was 1999 and religion in schools had become such a contentious issue in the 1970s and 1980s that our education systems had seemingly decided it was safest to have everyone check religion at the doors of the school and relegate practice, and even conversation, to the private sphere.

One of my first graduate school courses was Arabic I, and at the first session I was surprised when I learned that my professor was Muslim. I was at a Christian seminary! I was by no means upset, just surprised. I recall him saying good-naturedly one evening, "Just think, now every time you have a question in one of your Islamic Studies classes, you can ask me and you will impress your other professors with your use of primary sources!"

He was right. While I never became a proficient Arabic speaker, I benefited much more from the thought-provoking and compassionate conversations that took place between language drills. My professor encouraged us to ask him anything but noted that we should be willing to consider how we as Christians might answer the questions too. These personal interactions with the only real Muslim I knew at the time would forever shape the way I approached interfaith engagement in both the classroom and my personal life.

For the past ten years I have been teaching Islamic Studies at a private Christian university in classrooms that are exclusively composed of Christian students, most of them evangelicals. This is not always an easy audience. However, I have found that over and over again, there is power in stories and in face-to-face interaction. Ethnography and personal interviews shape my academic research and I want to make personal interaction and storytelling a central part of the classroom experience.

Hospitality, both in our actions as well as in our thinking, is a central theme of each of my courses on Islam. This takes on different forms depending on the class. Sometimes I invite students from the local Muslim student association to talk about what it's like to be a person of deep religious commitment on a college campus where you are a minority. Other times I invite Muslim women from different generations to come have tea with my female students and discuss their life experiences and how gender influences religious practice. In my course evaluations, students often comment that these interactions are the most meaningful days of the class, making the course material relevant, and as one student remarked, "touchable."

So I continue inviting Muslim students into my classes, not only because students consistently express how much they enjoy these interactions, but mainly because these interactions force my students (and myself) to demystify the idea of the "other" and recognize that all people are worthy of our hospitality and our empathy.

There is power in stories and in face-to-face interaction.

Sometimes we literally have to meet a Muslim neighbor in order to recognize that they are human. I feel privileged to be a part of these types of experiences.

At my university, I consistently tell students that we cannot interrogate others of different belief systems with questions we are not willing to ask ourselves. Recall, this is what was modeled for me by my Arabic teacher fifteen years ago. Also, as Christians we cannot hold others accountable to a different set of rules from the ones we choose to follow. As my relationships with the Muslim community grow, I feel consistently convicted to make sure that who I am and what I say does not change, regardless of who is in the audience. What I say about Islam needs to remain based in sound academic content and should not be manipulated to alleviate Christian insecurity.

We cannot interrogate others of different belief systems with questions we are not willing to ask ourselves.

While I want students (of all ages and in all environments) to be equipped with knowledge, I also want my students to become more confident in their own beliefs. This is not achieved through debunking or proving another religion wrong. Instead, if Christians are willing to ask themselves the same tough questions we ask of Muslims, we will allow for engagement in some very healthy (and needed) self-reflection. I am never more proud of students than when, after coming to the realization that we do a lot of things without knowing why, they seek to find answers in Scripture or in other sources. They realize that our answers do not mean much if they fail us once we move them beyond the confines of our own Christian tribe.

7

Inside the Bubble

SAMPLE LEARNING ACTIVITIES

We've explored the benefits of cultivating healthy learning spaces where persons who share religious beliefs can come together to challenge and support each other, so now it's time to get practical. If we're going to develop the skills necessary for constructive engagement with people who believe differently, we need to devote time to actually learning and practicing how to dialogue well. Loving our religious neighbors requires critical thinking skills and habits that enable us to see from different perspectives, listen charitably, process ideas independently and communally, and speak in a manner of collaboration rather than debate. For several years now we've been working with faculty, students, and staff at our Christian university to learn and practice these skills. In this chapter you'll find several practical activities that we've found useful.

COMMUNITY DAY: LEARNING TO DIALOGUE INSTEAD OF DEBATE

We all enter interfaith engagement from different starting points. We differ in degrees of religious literacy, social and emotional intelligence, personal experience with diverse people, and depth of critical thinking skill. Focusing on learning together as a community allows us to expand our horizons beyond what we would ever be able to accomplish as individuals. At the same time, learning as a community can itself be challenging and requires us to be intentional about treating each other with humility, hospitality, and respect.

Parker Palmer has long advocated the idea of creating and fostering communities of learners. According to Palmer, truth itself has a communal dimension and thus "require[s] many eyes and ears, many observations and experiences. . . . It require[s] a continual cycle of discussion, disagreement, and consensus over what has been seen and what it all means."[1] In order to cultivate truth in the context of a learning community, Palmer seeks to "take into account the larger community of truth in which . . . [students] live their lives."[2] This involves not only asking questions about factual content but also exploring the context in which that content emerges and the reality of the person encountering the content. Allowing space for questions also makes it safe for us to admit what we don't know and to be willing to make mistakes. Palmer puts it this way: "When people in a classroom begin to learn that every attempt at truth, no matter how off the mark, is a contribution to the larger search for corporate and consensus truth, they are soon emboldened and empowered to say what they need to say, to expose their ignorance."[3]

A major challenge to finding space for communal learning, however, is both the pace and the style with which we typically approach higher education. Often we find ourselves rushing from one class or meeting to the next class or meeting, one topic or idea to the next topic and idea. Rarely do we stop to assess how our thoughts about an issue have been percolating over time or to revisit an issue to explore the questions we now have about it. And the view that higher education exists solely for the purpose of transmitting knowledge and skills also works against the idea that community conversations are an important aspect of learning.

To address these challenges, we advocate the use of "community days" to create space for open conversation and dialogue. In the context of a classroom, for example, this can mean devoting one day every two weeks to discussion. On community day we assign no new material and cover no new content. We focus entirely on talking about ideas and questions that have emerged since the last community day. In order to implement effective and constructive community conversations, consider the following.

Establish community rules. Ground rules establish boundaries that help foster security and trust within the community conversation. The first activity you might consider using with a group in which difficult dialogues will be taking place is to have the group collaboratively develop and agree to its own set of rules. It can be helpful to look at existing lists of conversation guidelines for ideas to get this activity started.[4] Some sample rules could include:

- Speak honestly and openly.
- What is said in the room stays in the room.
- Avoid name-calling and stereotypes.
- Look for what's right and true, even in the views with which you disagree.
- Always show respect.

While ground rules are important, they aren't supposed to prevent disagreement or discomfort. The purpose of community day is not to have conversations that merely affirm what we hold in common and make us feel good about ourselves. Instead we need to challenge each other and be willing to challenge ourselves. This is hard work that can feel intimidating and upsetting—but it's necessary. Ground rules can help us avoid unnecessary hurt and help each participant feel empowered and safe. When we allow conversations to be difficult at times, we help to develop the skills needed for loving our religious neighbors well, even amid substantive differences.

Balance planned dialogue with open dialogue. In order to cultivate an effective community day, it's helpful to plan some initial questions or activities to get things started. This is especially true in contexts where deep and open dialogue hasn't been the norm. At the same time, don't allow community days to become too scripted. These conversations are intended to create an open-ended space of processing and discussing ideas. On community day the conversation is the end itself, not the means to meeting a content objective. Here are some ideas for launching effective community day conversations:

- *Ask participants to prepare beforehand.* For example, have each participant make a list of three readings, issues, comments, or questions that stand out from the previous two weeks. Or ask participants to identify the "muddiest point"—that is, the issue or reading that's still unclear or confusing. Another alternative is to have participants write a journal entry prior to the meeting, describing what they've been wondering about during the last two weeks. Community day can then begin by having participants share their prepared reflections, with conversation proceeding from there.

- *Invite participants to script the questions.* At the beginning of a community day, ask participants to work together in small groups to develop two or three questions they'd like the community to discuss together. Have each group share the questions and decide which to discuss together as a whole group.

- *Begin the meeting with an imaginative exercise.* A case study or role-playing activity (see pages 144-47), for example, might help participants integrate material from previous weeks into their assigned roles. This can also be an effective way to identify what lingering questions and concerns emerge. These questions and concerns can then become the basis for an open-ended community conversation.

Embrace the value of silence. As a rule, our classrooms, meetings, and clubs involve talking. Either someone is communicating information to the rest of the group or the group is discussing information that's been presented. Rarely do we sit together in silence. Not only does silence tend to make us feel uncomfortable, but we may also assume that silence is unproductive or that we simply don't have time for it because of the amount of material we think we need to cover. Palmer challenges us to consider the value of silence: "I think of silence as a tool of inquiry. . . . When we fall into silence in the classroom . . . the deepest possible thing may be happening—we may be thinking over or working our way through a problem or conundrum that we don't know the answer to."[5]

Silence is valuable in discussion for many reasons. First, it allows time for slower processors to gather their thoughts and identify their questions. This helps increase the likelihood that more people will have something to offer to the discussion. Silence also functions as an equalizer, helping to ensure that no one person dominates a conversation. Silence can also increase the quality and depth of thinking that takes place in a discussion. By utilizing silence to slow down the pace of processing, we provide participants with an opportunity to reflect on what questions, critiques, and comments would be most worthwhile to share with the group. In addition, silence can actually help the participants grow together as a community. In Palmer's words, "In silence you have a deeper sense of community or relationship than you sometimes have in the speaking of words."[6]

Here are suggestions to consider when implementing the practice of silence into community days:

- *Be transparent about your objectives.* In order to decrease the awkwardness surrounding silence in a discussion, explain why you're allowing time for quiet processing. For example, you might explain that silence is going to be used to give everyone time to process their thoughts carefully. Or you might describe that you want the community to experience sitting silently together. And within the context of a religious "bubble," silence can also be utilized to listen to God or meditate on Scripture before discussing an idea further.

• *Provide directions for the silence.* For example, say, "In order to give everyone time to process their thoughts carefully, let's sit with this idea for five minutes and then share what we believe are the most important insights or challenges raised by the idea." Or ask participants to write their thoughts quietly during this time and then prioritize their more important insights before deciding what to share with the group. You may even consider asking participants to sit quietly with no further directions, and then process together what that experience felt like and what was valuable about it.

• *Establish clear guidelines for participation frequency.* We're all aware that every group has participants who talk too much and participants who don't talk enough. Utilizing silence as part of discussion time can help create boundaries that establish more balanced participation. For example, participants can be told that everyone will be asked to share one idea after a time of silent reflection. This not only limits the amount of talking that some participants do; it also allows quiet or shy participants the opportunity to think through and prepare what they'll share.

The Doubting Game and the Believing Game: Learning to See from Different Perspectives

Higher education isn't doing its job if students (and faculty and staff) aren't developing and exhibiting skill in thinking. For many in academia and beyond, the word "thinking" is synonymous with "critical thinking"—that is, scrutinizing an idea with an eye toward finding its flaws. This is, of course, an important skill that absolutely should be fostered throughout a person's education and practiced in life after college. Educator and literary scholar Peter Elbow refers to this type of thinking as the "doubting game," in which we "scrutinize with the tool of doubt," approaching an idea skeptically and analytically.[7] Such a practice, he argues, doesn't involve rejecting everything; rather, in the doubting game, we test ideas through "systematic skepticism" in order to see "which ideas are more worth trusting."[8]

Applying this thinking tool to interfaith engagement, some might assume that the "tool of doubt" is exactly what we need to use when considering the religious ideas of others. After all, some Christian educators might argue, students need to learn to reject religious falsehood so they can embrace the truth. While we recognize this, we also know that each of us unintentionally clings to some erroneous beliefs—about our own faith as well as about the faith of others—and this is where the doubting game can be particularly useful. Playing the doubting game, observes Elbow, helps reveal "hidden contradictions, bad reasoning, or other weaknesses . . . , especially in the case of ideas that seem true or attractive."[9] In fact, he continues, the purpose of "systematic skepticism is to try to doubt what we find most obvious or true or right."[10] If we hope to learn to think well about faith, we need to be willing to submit even our dearest ideas to rigorous examination and critique—to play the doubting game.

At the same time, the doubting game is only half of the picture. Of equal importance in learning to think well is the "believing game," which Elbow defines as "the disciplined practice of trying to be as welcoming or accepting as possible" to ideas that are different from our own.[11] In the believing game, we aren't merely tolerating an idea or a person advocating this idea, keeping our mouths shut for the sake of politeness. Instead, we're test-driving an idea, entering into it, seeking to see from the vantage point of a person who advocates this idea, hoping thereby to experience "a kind of conditional or temporary believing."[12]

Such an exercise in provisional belief can be useful in many ways. First of all, trying out different ways of thinking or points of view can help us find flaws in our own thinking and reveal things we unconsciously take for granted.[13] This is an important exercise because most of us aren't very good at self-critique, particularly when it comes to ideas that are centrally important to us (such as religious beliefs). Thus, the believing game becomes a valuable tool by getting us inside another perspective so that we can then "look back from there at one's own view—from the outside."[14] Second, because the believing game forces us to spend time inside an idea, it can help us see when "there are certain conditions or certain senses in which [that idea] makes sense."[15] Third, our willingness to participate in the believing game shows our willingness to try to understand our neighbors as best we can, "to invest or insert ourselves" in their beliefs and practices rather than simply dismiss them out of hand.[16]

Ideas for playing the believing game.

- The group leader introduces the idea of the doubting and believing game, ensuring participants that ideas will have time to be both "believed" and "doubted." Telling participants that this is a game also helps to allay fears by emphasizing the provisional nature of both assent and critique.

- At some point during discussion, a group leader enforces a time of listening in which no one may argue his or her own point without first restating the perspective of another to that person's satisfaction.[17]

- Particularly when considering a perspective that initially seems problematic, participants can be encouraged to try to "tell a story of someone who believes [this idea]," working to "imagine and describe someone who sees things this way" and to consider what "events might have led people to have this view of the world."[18]

• Participants who object to an exercise that asks them to "believe" a perspective with which they disagree strenuously might be willing to take part if they understand that the believing game can also help reveal some of the experiences that have shaped another person's belief.[19] Gaining such understanding of and empathy for others is surely a goal that all can support.

• If discussion gets heated, or if participants are clearly having trouble understanding and considering a particular perspective, "the objectors need to stop talking and simply give extended floor time to the minority view" for a while.[20] This can be accomplished through a time of "allies only—no objections" in which only those who are "having more success believing or entering into or assenting to the minority view" may speak.[21]

LEARNING TO LISTEN: PRACTICING THE PRINCIPLE OF CHARITY

We all have much to learn if we hope to show love to our religious neighbors. Particularly for those Christians from traditions with a strong evangelistic emphasis, listening to one's religious neighbor (rather than always seeking to speak) can present a challenge. Yet developing the skill of charitable and empathetic listening is essential for healthy interfaith engagement.

Genuine listening means seeking to understand first. We should always try to see another's perspective in the best light possible, before commenting on or critiquing that view. Often we spend so much time in a conversation thinking about what we're going to say next that we fail to hear what the other person is actually saying. Learning to listen charitably means allowing myself to hear the position actually being articulated so that I can go on to form a wiser, more thoughtful, and better-reasoned opinion of that view.

Many Christians approach religious others with preconceived or stereotypical ideas about why the other religion is flawed, leading them to assume that other religious believers are simply misguided. Learning to listen helps move the conversation away from an argumentative focus that attempts to prove the other position wrong toward the goals of empathy and understanding. This shift in attitude toward interaction with our religious neighbors lessens the likelihood that hasty assumptions will lead to misunderstanding. And it helps us extend the benefit of the doubt to the other, recognizing that she probably has very good reasons for her beliefs.

In order to cultivate the skill of charitable listening, each of us needs to approach the other with an open mind. Questions such as "What does this view get right about the world?" "What beliefs or values do I share in common with this person?" and "What about her views do I find persuasive?" are helpful for shifting our attitude from one of argument and debate to one of listening and understanding. Asking these sorts of questions also helps slow down the conversation, delaying our response time and ensuring that we have worked to understand and find common ground before focusing on a critique of our differences.

According to the mutual inquiry model of Wayne Booth, teaching students "how to be persuaded" is as essential a critical and civic capacity as teaching them "how to persuade."[22] Booth suggests that this can be accomplished by teaching students how to listen, a goal accomplished through approaches such as Elbow's believing game. The believing game deepens listening by requiring not just listening to views different from our own without argument, not just trying to restate these ideas without bias, but "actually trying to believe them."[23] Such listening encourages students to "take seriously claims they might otherwise dismiss" and "discover some of the experiences that have shaped a classmate's belief on some issue."[24]

One strategy that we've developed and utilized in order to teach charitable listening is an assignment that we call "Learning to Listen." We've modified this assignment to fit a variety of situations, from introductory explorations to upper-level courses. While this assignment was designed for classroom use, it could easily be adapted for a campus club, church group, or other informal setting. (For example, participants may come prepared to share their findings at a club meeting instead of preparing a written assignment.) Additionally, notice in the description that we've designed this assignment so that it strongly encourages students to participate in at least one out-of-class interfaith dialogue, but the assignment doesn't absolutely require this. Participants who haven't had much experience in diverse settings may prefer to practice their charitable listening skills with an idea they encounter in a film or text before they begin interacting with persons of different faiths. Here is how we often describe the Learning to Listen project to our students:

Learning to Listen project. Learning to Listen is a two-part project in which you first collect and report on information and then reflect on that information. This project asks you to think and engage personally about living as a Christian in a diverse world by interacting with and reflecting on a religious tradition different from your own.

Part one: Collecting and reporting on information. For each of the options listed below, you'll research and report on an aspect of a religious tradition that isn't familiar to you—another Christian tradition (such as Pentecostalism, Catholicism, or Anglicanism) or another religion (such as Judaism, Islam, or Hinduism). You may choose the particular focus of this research. For example, perhaps you're interested in how members of this religious tradition view a particular issue, like war, sexuality, or racial reconciliation. Or

perhaps you're interested in learning more about the spiritual practices of this particular tradition, like religious worship, or spiritual
disciplines, such as fasting or meditation. Whatever topic you
choose, be sure to select sources that are academically credible and
appropriate. This means they must have been published in a repu-
table journal or book.

- *Option one:* Minimum of eight academically credible and topic-
  appropriate sources.

- *Option two:* Minimum of five academically credible and topic-
  appropriate sources; participate in one interfaith dialogue.

- *Option three:* Minimum of two academically credible and topic-
  appropriate sources; participate in two interfaith dialogues.

- *Option four:* Participate in three or more interfaith dialogues.

For each source, include a 200-word summary of information
gained from the source. In this portion of the project you're simply
reporting on information as clearly and accurately as you can.

Part 2: Reflecting on information. The primary purpose of
this portion of the project is for you to react to and reflect personally on something you learned through the information-
collection phase of the project. This is not merely a research
paper where you report factual information. Instead this is a reflection paper, where you articulate and develop your thoughts
about what you've researched. In your paper you should address
the following questions, although you don't have to address them
in any particular order and you may choose to give different emphasis to each:

- *At least 500 words:* How might a believer from your tradition
  relate to and learn productively from the beliefs and practices of
  the religious tradition you learned about in this project? (In
  other words, where is there commonality?)

- *At least 500 words:* Did you feel separate from or disagree with the religious tradition you learned about in this project? You might reflect here on beliefs and practices you learned about. (If you didn't feel separate from or disagree with the tradition you learned about, then use this portion of your paper to explore questions or concerns that were raised for you through your research or participation in the interfaith dialogues.)

- *At least 300 words:* What general conclusions do you draw from this project about the opportunities, challenges, and responsibilities of living as a Christian in a diverse world?

- *At least 300 words:* What else would you like to say about your experience doing this project?

IMAGINATION CULTIVATION: PROCESSING IN DIFFERENT CONTEXTS

In chapter five we discussed the importance of cultivating imaginative empathy to enable us to better understand another person's story. Imagination is important because it helps us develop compassion, and compassion in turn leads to a greater sense of civic responsibility.[25] Loving our religious neighbors well requires embracing the humanity of the other and seeking to understand her perspectives as much as possible—and this takes imagination, as we picture ourselves in her story. In so doing we may not change our own beliefs, but we do seek to "widen [our] appreciation for ways of life different than [our] own."[26] Such imaginative activity can also help us better evaluate both the strengths and limitations of our own stories.[27]

While imagination is indispensible in our cultivation of empathy and in our critical self-examination, it also helps us learn to see ourselves and others in new ways, along with the possibilities for peaceful relationships together. These insights are crucial for helping us begin to develop a vision that is "capable of giving birth to that which does not exist."[28] This vision is what John Paul Lederach seeks to cultivate in his extensive peace-building work in areas around the globe marred by violence. As we strive for civic peace and harmony amid hostility, we need to develop an imagination that enables us to see ourselves in a web of relationships with others, even those who are our enemies. This makes it more difficult for us to draw sharp divides between "us" and "them"—divides that allow difference and misunderstanding to harden into hatred and violence. Additionally, notes Lederach, peace-building relies on our ability to imagine solutions to seemingly intractable problems.

There are several ways to cultivate imagination in classrooms and small group discussions. These activities can be useful to employ both before and after interfaith engagement activities. The goal is to "create space for temporary suspension of deliberation and judgment"[29] where students can practice imagining the world from another's perspective along with ways to communicate their own beliefs and values with others. In each case it's important to remember the value of cultivating a supportive space to learn together, as discussed in chapter six. Below are some suggestions for activities that help cultivate an empathetic imagination.

Case studies. Case studies are common pedagogical tools used to help develop the capacity to think from multiple perspectives. In the context of developing skills for interfaith engagement, case studies help us envision multiple paths to civic harmony (as well as recognize the potential obstacles to peace), learn to see the humanity of all people as we each make decisions rooted in our own faith and values, and accept the good reasons different people have for their beliefs. Case studies also help us imagine options and compromises we may not have previously realized.

Michael Stoltzfus and James Reffel have found case studies to be an effective and practical method for building imaginative empathy.

Case studies, they observe, are useful because they "strongly emphasize the connections between belief and practice; ideas and their consequences; arguments and their embodiment. Empathy, imagination, and curiosity develop as students wrestle with situations, hear peers raise questions, and struggle with uncertainty."[30] Case studies involve fictional or real-world scenarios where participants study different sides of an issue and work together to solve a problem. By presenting instances of religious diversity that lead to either conflict or cooperation, case studies are particularly instructive for helping participants better understand the ways in which those involved in that situation played a role "in either fanning the flames of conflict or building the bridges of cooperation."[31] This understanding then helps cultivate the ability to imagine alternative outcomes.

When using case studies in discussion, consider the following suggestions:[32]

• *Find a current event where tensions around religious diversity play a central role in the issue at stake.* Ideally, look for a case where participants will be able to identify with the context, making it easier to imagine having a stake in what's decided. For example, choose an event from your own city or state to bring the problem closer or utilize a case involving communities or contexts similar to your own.

• *Research what's at stake for the different representatives in the case study.* What outcomes are they hoping to achieve? What motivates them to hold their respective positions? Or you might assign participants to research different sides of the issue prior to discussion, allowing the group itself to develop the case study.

• *Have participants read the case study and discuss it together.* Some questions could include: How would I feel if I were from religious tradition x, y, or z? How is the community as a whole impacted by the decisions made? What decisions would promote civic harmony? What decisions would create further conflict? What would it mean to love your religious neighbor in this situation?

Role-playing. Current educational research suggests that learning increases when assignments are connected to "real world" activities that have a defined audience and clear task.[33] Situating discussions about interfaith engagement within a realistic context can be much more effective than having abstract, thesis-driven debates. Utilizing role-playing as a discussion tool, for example, helps develop the capacity to imagine ourselves in concrete situations where we have to decide how to respond and interact with others. Role-playing also provides a safe space to develop the skills we need in order to show love to our religious neighbors.

Role-playing can take place as a face-to-face conversational activity where some group members observe the role-play in action, with the whole group then discussing this experience. Or role-playing can involve writing activities that help prepare participants for discussion by allowing everyone individual time to process their ideas, questions, and concerns. Some sample activities include:

- *Imagine you've been asked to speak at your church about the importance of loving our religious neighbors.* Some members of your church question whether this is consistent with Christian belief and practice. Describe why you think interfaith engagement is important and explain how it fits within the specific context of your denomination or tradition.[34] What objections might be raised and how would you respond to them?

- *Imagine that you're going to be participating in an interfaith event where you'll be asked to share your faith story with those who may not be familiar with Christianity.* The point of this event isn't evangelism but rather to build greater understanding of different religions through personal storytelling, so share a narrative that would help someone else see the world through your eyes. You might consider focusing on one or two personal experiences that help explain why you're a Christian or how you practice your faith on a daily basis. Or you might choose to focus on one or two Christian values and teachings that are particularly important to you.

- *Imagine that you're going to be interviewing a person from a different religious background.* Develop a set of interview questions intended to help you understand how the world looks through her or his eyes. Be sure to consider the importance of humility and empathy as you draft your questions and consider how your questions will be heard and interpreted by the other person.

Spiritual autobiography. Nussbaum emphasizes the important role that literature can play in helping to develop our imaginative capacities by cultivating "sensitivity and judgment that inform moral and political choices" and helping us understand the choices that others make as well.[35] Religion could easily be added to this list of choices, and spiritual autobiographies are a powerful way to help us learn to interact well with people who believe differently, before actually leaving the safety and support of our own religious communities. Stoltzfus and Reffel's work supports these claims, demonstrating that reading religious autobiographies helps us to "appreciate how a diversity of traditions are able to inspire the human qualities of hope, humility, faith, commitment, and love" and help us to recognize our own limited perspectives.[36]

Ultimately, once we understand that "moral responsibility and human compassion transcend particular religious affiliations," we can "respond to distinct religious worldviews with empathy and curiosity."[37] Encountering different spiritual autobiographies also begins to cultivate some of the religious literacy we need in order to imagine another person's world. It reminds us that a single story can

provide only one view of a particular religion, and it helps us begin
to think about how we might share our own spiritual narratives.

We recommend the following autobiographies as a starting place.
Each was chosen for its focus on navigating one's personal beliefs
and values in the midst of other religious perspectives.

- Saleemah Abdul-Ghafur, ed., *Living Islam Out Loud: American Muslim Women Speak* (Boston: Beacon Press, 2012). This series of essays, by women who identify as both Muslim and American, explores the tensions between religion, culture, ethnicity, and gender woven through their lives. The book includes personal reflections and poems on topics such as hijab, sexuality, relationships, and spirituality.

- Paul Cowan, *An Orphan in History: Retrieving a Jewish Legacy* (New York: William Morrow, 1996). This is the story of the author's journey from assimilated American secular Jew toward a deliberate, observant Jewish life in America. Of particular relevance for Christian readers are his stories of anti-Semitism, of Christian privilege, and of disagreements about what it might look like to be religiously faithful in a secular society.

- Dennis Covington, *Salvation on Sand Mountain* (New York: Penguin, 1995). The author describes the personal impact of time spent with Pentecostal Christians in Appalachia. These encounters with significant difference in theology and practice cause him to recognize the appeal of this community in a way that leads to a reassessment of his own belief and practice.

- Ali Eteraz, *Children of Dust: A Portrait of a Muslim as a Young Man* (New York: HarperOne, 2011). In this memoir, the author describes the development of his own personal and spiritual identity. Born in Pakistan to a father who promised Allah his son would be a great leader of Islam, Eteraz moves to the United States at age ten. This book recounts how he has navigated the intersections of culture and religion, ultimately arriving at a place of spiritual awakening.

- Ranya Tabari Idliby, *Burqas, Baseball, and Apple Pie* (New York: Palgrave Macmillan, 2014). The author's many personal stories—particularly those in which she responds to questions from her children—provide an interesting, informative, and intimate picture of what it's like to be a Muslim in America today.

- Thich Nhat Hanh, *Living Buddha, Living Christ* (New York: Penguin, 1995). The author, a Buddhist monk, uses short meditative reflections to describe how his faith has been shaped by a contemplative study of the lives and teachings of both Buddha and Christ. He stresses the importance of interfaith dialogue as a way to find peace, mutual understanding, and common ground between different religions.

- Maria Poggi Johnson, *Strangers and Neighbors: What I Have Learned About Christianity by Living among Orthodox Jews* (Nashville: Thomas Nelson, 2004). The author, professor of theology and a Catholic, describes the ways in which her own Christian faith has been changed through time spent getting to know her Orthodox Jewish neighbors. She reflects on commonalities as well as differences that challenge her.

- Michael Muhammed Knight, *Impossible Man* (New York: Soft Skull Press, 2009). In this coming-of-age memoir, Knight tells the story of his adolescent conversion to Islam. His spiritual life develops within a complex web of a mentally ill father, reading Malcolm X, a trip to Pakistan, and various aspects of American pop culture.

- Eboo Patel, *Acts of Faith* (Boston: Beacon, 2007). The founder of Interfaith Youth Core tells the story of ways in which his friendships with people of other faiths led both to his own spiritual reawakening and to his desire to promote interfaith cooperation, particularly among college students.

- Jennifer Howe Peace, Or N. Rose, and Gregory Mobley, eds., *My Neighbor's Faith* (Maryknoll, NY: Orbis, 2012). This collection contains more than fifty accounts of meaningful interfaith encounters told by people from many faith traditions. Each story is brief and accessible, focusing on an unexpected insight that the author gained through this encounter.

- Patricia Raybon and Alana Raybon, *Undivided: A Muslim Daughter, Her Christian Mother, and Their Path to Peace* (Nashville: Thomas Nelson, 2015). Written as a series of alternating narratives between mother and daughter, this book focuses on family members divided by faith who seek to find common ground and understanding despite their differences in belief and practice.

- Kevin Roose, *The Unlikely Disciple: A Sinner's Semester at America's Holiest University* (New York: Grand Central Publishing, 2009). The author, a Brown University sophomore, gives an account of a semester spent as a student at a conservative Christian university (Liberty University). Both respectful and willing to criticize, the author's story of his experiences provides useful insights from an informed outsider.

- Chris Stedman, *Faitheist: How an Atheist Found Common Ground with the Religious* (Boston: Beacon Press, 2012). Stedman recounts his own journey from Christianity to atheism, sharing how his experiences with intolerance and lack of love on both sides of this faith line eventually led him to become a bridge-builder. This honest and thought-provoking narrative challenges many stereotypes and assumptions about secular humanism and inspires readers to forge partnerships where religious and non-religious persons can work together for the common good.

- Krista Tippett, *Speaking of Faith* (New York: Viking, 2007). The author, whose radio program by the same name (now called *On Being*), draws on her own life story as well as interviews she has conducted. The insights she has gained provide many thought-provoking reflections into the human condition as well as the importance of taking time to really listen to one another.

- G. Willow Wilson, *The Butterfly Mosque: A Young American Woman's Journey to Love and Islam* (New York: Grove Press, 2011). Wilson, a white American living in Egypt, tells the story of her conversion to Islam and her marriage to a Muslim man. Provides numerous insights about the complexities and joys of learning to navigate a new culture and religion.

- Lauren Winner, *Girl Meets God: On the Path to a Spiritual Life* (New York: Shaw Books, 2004). The author tells the story of her two religious conversions—first to Judaism, a community with which she found real belonging and a faith whose observances she found deeply meaningful, then to Christianity, a shift that she found initially difficult as she struggled to determine how much of her Jewish self she would have to leave behind.

- Lauren Winner, *Mudhouse Sabbath* (Brewster, MA: Paraclete Press, 2003). Having converted from Judaism to Christianity, Winner explores her religious roots by applying Jewish spiritual practices to the life of a Christian believer. Covering a spectrum of topics from fasting and sabbath to prayer and aging, this book provides a model for how one's own faith can be strengthened by learning the teachings of another faith.

Films and television

- *30 Days: Muslims and America* (season one, episode three). In this documentary by Morgan Spurlock (*Supersize Me*) a Christian man agrees to live with a Muslim family for thirty days. The film provides interviews with this man and with members of the family he spends time with that month.

- *An American Mosque* (2012). Set in rural California, this documentary tells the story of a community's response to a religiously motivated hate crime against local Muslims.

- *Arranged* (2007). This story centers on the friendship between an Orthodox Jewish woman and a Muslim woman who meet as first-year teachers at a public school in Brooklyn. As they get to know each other, they see that they have much in common—including that both are going through the process of arranged marriages.

- *Between Allah and Me (and Everyone Else)* (2015). This documentary explores the challenges that four Muslim women living in North America face when they decide to start (or stop) wearing the hijab.

- *Different Books, Common Word* (2009). This documentary focuses on some Baptists and some Muslims from several cities in the United States who are working together to find common ground through exploring the command in both traditions to love one's neighbor.

- *Divided We Fall: Americans in the Aftermath* (2006). This thought-provoking documentary was prompted by the brutal murder of a Sikh man in the aftermath of 9/11.

- *Encounter Point* (2006). This documentary follows peace activists Ali Abu Awwad and Robi Damelin, who work together in Israel/Palestine.

- *Fordson: Faith, Fasting, Football* (2011). This documentary follows a predominantly Arab-American high school football team preparing for a big game during the final days of Ramadan. It provides a picture of a community seeking to be faithful Muslims while also hoping for acceptance in America.

- *Hiding and Seeking* (2005). The filmmaker (Menachem Daum) is an Orthodox Jew from New York City. Hoping to convince his sons that Jews and Gentiles ought to work together, they travel together to Poland in search of the family who saved their grand-father and his brothers from the Holocaust.

- *The Imam and the Pastor* (2009). This documentary focuses on two Nigerians who fought on opposing sides during religious conflict in their country—Imam Muhammad Ashafa and Pastor James Wuye. It shows their change of heart and the reconciliation efforts in which they have been involved.

- *Mariam* (2016). Mariam is a French-born Muslim girl with Arab parents. Her decision to start wearing the hijab poses problems for her in the wake of French laws banning religious symbols in public schools.

- *Mooz-Lum* (2010). The main character, raised in a strict Muslim family, has just begun fitting into his new college community when the 9/11 attacks force difficult choices on him.

- *My So-Called Enemy* (2010). This documentary is a coming-of-age story about six young women from Israel/Palestine who participate in a program called Building Bridges for Peace. Of particular interest are their struggles to reconcile this transformative experience with the realities of conflict-filled life in the Middle East.

- *New Muslim Cool* (2009). This documentary tells the story of a Puerto Rican American rapper whose past life as a drug dealer was turned around when he converted to Islam. Now he's trying to use his actions and his music as a force for good, motivated by his Muslim faith.

- *Of Gods and Men* (2010). Based on a true story, this film explores a group of Christian monks in an impoverished community in North Africa who must decide whether to stay or leave in response to threats from fundamentalist terrorists.

- *The Quarrel* (1991). In this film two estranged friends, Hersh and Chaim, discuss their views of God in post-Holocaust Montreal.

Hersh has remained a devout Jew and Rabbi, while Chaim is now an agnostic. Despite their significant ideological differences, they remain committed to dialogue and the possibility of friendship.

CONCLUSION

"Bubbles" aren't entirely bad. They're important spaces where we can challenge and support each other to develop the receptive humility, reflective commitment, and imaginative empathy needed to love our religious neighbors well. But we must also remember that bubbles are limited spaces where "oversimplification becomes the almost inevitable outcome."[38] Thus, it's also important that we leave our bubbles, entering unfamiliar neighborhoods and worship spaces. In the next chapter we provide practical resources for building healthy and constructive relationships with those who believe differently.

TALK ABOUT IT

- What do you think are the most important guidelines or rules to establish before engaging in interfaith conversations?

- What is the value of silence? How might you benefit from more silence during discussion in your classes or meetings?

- What is the role of imagination in peace-building? What are some areas where your own imagination needs to be cultivated?

GIVE IT A TRY

Read one of the spiritual autobiographies or watch one of the films listed in this chapter. Then discuss how your imaginative empathy was cultivated by encountering this story.

WHY I'M GLAD I SKIPPED LARGE GROUP

Greg Damhorst, IFYC alum, cofounder of Faith Line Protestants

I always thought my undergraduate life was exactly what my parents had hoped it would be. I was a premed physics major, I trained as an EMT, I volunteered at a local clinic, and I was active in a large Christian fellowship in which I led a Bible study. I imagine they felt some degree of relief that I hadn't used my newfound freedom as a college student at a large state university to distance myself from the Christian life they had raised me to follow. In fact, I stuck to the prescribed regimen: dedicated student, volunteer, leader.

But despite the way my resume looked, something wasn't right. On Thursday nights I attended "large group" as part of my Christian fellowship, the main event after a week of leadership team meetings, small group planning, community-building, discipleship, and Bible study. Thursday nights were usually expected to be the highlight of the week for all of us, especially student leaders.

Those Thursday nights impacted my life significantly, but not because of what I found at large group. As I would reach for the door to our meeting place right off a main street in our campus town, someone would be there, sitting on the ground next to that door. He remained nameless and faceless, sitting in front of a Christian fellowship meeting space between a bar and a liquor store on a street that would soon be swarming with students. He was unkempt and dirty, often asking for money. Occasionally in the cold. Always alone.

And every Thursday I walked past. Up the stairs to be a Bible study leader, to join a hundred other Christian college students who would pass by on their way to large group. There we would sing songs about God's compassion and strategize about how to get our nonbelieving friends to investigate the Bible. We would talk about social justice. We would pray that we would become world changers.

Tension grew in me every time I ignored that man on the street. I was being told to invite others into a relationship with God, yet increasingly I imagined that this very God would rather have skipped large group than ignore the man on the street. A lifelong evangelical, I believed I was mandated to communicate my faith to others. But could I really invite a friend to walk past the man on the street in order to hear a message about how God is compassionate?

When Jesus talked about a man attacked by robbers on the road from Jerusalem to Jericho in Luke 10:29-37, he described the Samaritan who stopped to help, saying, "Go and do likewise." But first he pointed out the priest and Levite who passed on the other side, avoiding the man in need. Perhaps they, like me, were also on their way to fulfill the obligation of their religious leadership.

This is not where my story of interfaith engagement begins, but it is where it becomes an essential part of my faith journey. Three years earlier, as a freshman, a friend had invited me to be a part of an interfaith dialogue and service group, and I had participated ever since. This really became meaningful, however, when I was no longer doing interfaith activities in spite of being an evangelical and started doing them because I was an evangelical.

Soon I stopped skipping service projects to go to Bible study and instead started skipping Bible study to go to service projects. There I joined Hindus, Muslims, Jews, Buddhists, Baha'i, and atheists in serving my community. The intentional interfaith atmosphere created dialogue on topics like "Why do you serve?" and I would share what I believed about how God intended the world to be, how the sacrifice of Jesus was a part of repairing the brokenness of the world, and how I believed I was called to participate in that process through serving others and spreading the gospel.

From these interactions I would return to the Bible to better know my own tradition and better understand this Jesus I was claiming to follow. Meanwhile I would learn about other traditions and find common ground with them, such as the Jewish concept of Tikkun Olam or the Jain notion that "rendering help to another is the function of all human beings." For perhaps the first time in my life, I met people of very different worldviews who were genuinely interested in what I had to say about my faith—and I didn't feel awkward talking to them about it.

As I began graduate school on the same campus, my search for a Christian community became driven by this perspective. I found a church that didn't ask me to ignore need in my community to follow a program agenda. Rather, I found a community where opening the doors of a food pantry to anyone in the community was a main part of its agenda. Building on the success of a massive food-packaging project created by our interfaith student group in undergrad, I founded a student organization supported by my church, which in less than four years has provided nearly 350,000 pounds of food to agencies throughout the state of Illinois, including over 1.5 million servings of a boil-and-eat rice-soy casserole.

That program has brought together over 12,000 individuals from a range of traditions as well as schools, educational institutions, and community organizations. We've collaborated extensively with a local Jewish temple and a Unitarian Universalist congregation, and we've hosted an annual service project on September 11 to bring students of different faith traditions together. We organize an annual service event so large that only the football stadium on campus makes an adequate venue. Along the way we have repeatedly challenged participants to share with each other: "Why do you serve?"

For me, this has not been a program about proselytizing but rather about communicating my faith through both words and actions. It has been about noticing the man on the side of the road and stopping, then asking others to help as well, and having a conversation about why we stopped—even if it means skipping large group.

> **For perhaps the first time in my life, I met people of very different worldviews who were genuinely interested in what I had to say about my faith—and I didn't feel awkward talking to them about it.**

8

Interfaith Engagement
Beyond the Bubble

While much learning can and does take place inside the classroom, learning opportunities "beyond the bubble" are essential for preparing Christians to constructively engage a religiously diverse world. This should come as no surprise. Educators have long believed that getting off campus contributes significantly to the learning process. And social psychologists have long argued that putting persons from different backgrounds in a common setting can erase prejudice.

Although most Christians are willing to participate in crosscultural learning, many still hesitate to embrace interfaith engagement. But moving beyond our religious bubbles is essential for pursuing civic harmony and loving our neighbors. Getting off campus allows us to get to know and interact with people who are genuinely committed to a different religion. Such interaction is important, say Douglas and Rhonda Jacobsen, because it allows us to get to know a religion "as it is actually lived, . . . to understand how that religion 'works' for the people involved in it."[1] And getting off campus shifts the power base. We experience what it's like to be the "other" in someone else's religious home. This cultivates a lived empathy that goes beyond what can be developed through books and films alone.

In the introduction to this book, we told a story about a time when we and our students attended an interfaith dialogue at a local mosque. There we listened to three religious leaders from different traditions discuss the topic of conversion. The Christian representative on the panel advocated a contextual view of missions, maintaining that a person can come to embrace Christianity without rejecting all that she's previously known and valued in her home culture and her home religion. Hearing this position alone challenged many of our students, as they worried that he may have compromised too much of the gospel in his efforts to respect other cultures and religions. Then the representatives from other faith traditions began to express in strong terms that they were deeply offended by this Christian panelist because he made it clear that he believes Christ to be *the* way and truth. Several of our students were shocked and confused, not sure whether they should feel angry and defensive or guilty and ashamed. The significant learning that took place in this single evening simply wouldn't have happened if we'd never left the bubble of our evangelical Christian campus community. At this event we heard a wide range of views expressed that we simply don't encounter on our campus. Most significantly, we had the lived experience of hearing these views in real time, in a setting where we weren't in charge.

Face-to-face encounters with embodied persons in unfamiliar territory make a significantly greater impact on us than ideas voiced through a text or film. First, being off campus puts us in a setting where we have the opportunity to show humility and practice hospitality by being good guests, receiving the hospitality of others. Walking into a new place for the first time, we naturally seek to show respect, patience, kindness, and generosity to our hosts. These attitudes help us to be more receptive listeners and humble learners. Second, physically inhabiting a space that makes us feel awkward and uncertain can lead us to respond differently than we might in a

familiar classroom setting. Instead of taking on an attitude of debate
and voicing our default perspectives, when we're off campus, we
realize that we need to listen quietly before responding. Unlike our
experiences when reading, watching a film, or surfing the Internet,
we can't simply disengage; we're face to face with difference and have
to practice the skills of balancing receptive humility with reflective
commitment. Third, encountering religious difference in unfamiliar
places teaches us important lessons about privilege and responsibility. When we're in a setting where we are the minority, or at least
not a strong majority, we begin to develop empathy for what it feels
like to be in the minority position. This cultivates a sense of responsibility for extending hospitality and giving voice to others.

At times being off campus means we're in situations where
others attempt to convert us to their religion, which isn't a common
experience for many Christians and doesn't happen on our over-
whelmingly Christian campus. This switch of role and change of
power dynamics teaches multiple lessons. Not only does this encourage empathy for anyone in the position of being proselytized,
it also creates complexity and humility as we think about how
Christianity relates to other religions.

When we heard a lecture at the Minnesota Da'wah Institute—a
center dedicated to teaching Islam and committed to proselytizing
in the name of Allah—about why we should be Muslim instead of
Christian, we and our students quickly learned that persons from
other faith traditions have very strong reasons for their beliefs and
aren't easily swayed by the challenges or questions we might pose.
We also learned that others have very developed intellectual arguments for not being Christian. This didn't lead our students to
abandon their faith. Instead it helped cultivate a mutual understanding between themselves and their Muslim peers.

We believe it's essential for Christians to engage with persons of
other religious traditions in a variety of settings, because this activity

cultivates the civic capacities needed to address the challenges of today and to meet Christ's commandment to love our neighbors. These experiences help prepare college students in particular for future service in any career. The challenges and opportunities of religious diversity in our society are undeniable and we must prepare Christians to be constructive partners in this context. In this chapter we offer some suggestions for building external partnerships with persons of other faiths, provide several examples of bridge-crossing projects and activities to consider using, and conclude with an annotated bibliography of helpful readings along these lines.

FINDING PARTNERS

Although the interfaith session on conversion provided an important learning moment for us and for our students, this type of event isn't necessarily ideal for achieving the goals we seek to meet through interfaith engagement. Extensive research on interfaith engagement among college students has found that "peer socialization is a vital component" for developing a pluralist attitude toward religious diversity.[2] The pluralist attitude defined by this study is a form of civic (but not necessarily theological) pluralism characterized by "migration from tolerance to acceptance of others" and by "understanding and appreciation of worldview differences (not merely commonalities)."[3] Perhaps surprisingly, this research suggests that curricular exposure to diversity doesn't do much in developing such pluralism. Instead, it's interactions with friends and peers that "bear the strongest relationship to pluralism orientation."[4]

In cultivating the sorts of experiences that help our students, and ourselves, build bridges with persons from different faith traditions, we need to heed the words of Rockenbach and her coauthors: "Inclusivity is crucial. We challenge educators to frame inter-worldview

exchanges so they have wider appeal and are inviting to students of
a wide array of religious, spiritual, and nonreligious worldviews."[5]
But many Christian college campuses and student groups aren't
that diverse. So below are a few suggestions for identifying external
partners in our interfaith work.

Interfaith Youth Core. Interfaith Youth Core (IFYC) is arguably
the leader in developing, training, and implementing interfaith engagement on college campuses. IFYC seeks to bring people of diverse religious and nonreligious identities together in order to accomplish its mission of making interfaith cooperation a cultural
norm. IFYC's particular focus within the context of higher education is driven by the belief that "American college students, supported by their campuses, can be the interfaith leaders we need to
make religion a bridge and not a barrier."[6]

Following the best practices advocated by research, many of
IFYC's programs focus on planning effective opportunities for
college students of different faiths to learn and serve together.
Better Together is IFYC's network through which students can
pursue the goal of interfaith cooperation by establishing campus
chapters and sharing resources and ideas with other campus
chapters. Better Together groups aren't limited to campuses with a
great deal of religious diversity. For example, at our Christian university, the Better Together club meets to promote intrafaith cooperation as well as to develop networks with groups on other campuses in order to reach a more religiously diverse pool of peers.

In addition to Better Together, IFYC provides a spectrum of resources designed to help students (and the faculty or staff who
support these students) develop the skills needed to become interfaith leaders. Each year IFYC hosts an Interfaith Leadership Institute that trains students, faculty, and staff from a wide range of
schools across the country to effectively address and engage religious diversity. At these institutes participants have the opportunity

to learn strategies, discuss challenges and resources, develop plans for their campus, and network with other campuses. IFYC also supports campuses in developing curricular programs in the emerging academic field of interfaith studies. And an extensive set of up-to-date resources for curricular and cocurricular event planning are available at no charge on IFYC's website. Campuses may also hire IFYC to do a specific assessment and consultation of the needs and assets of their own particular community.

Other campuses. External partnerships can also be developed in cooperation with other campuses. For example, over the years our students, faculty, and staff at Bethel have partnered with groups such as the Multifaith Alliance at Hamline University and the Al-Madinah Cultural Center (a Muslim student group) at the University of Minnesota. Many campuses have student religious organizations representing a wide range of faiths, and many have groups dedicated specifically to interfaith cooperation. Both the Better Together network and Campus Compact are resources to consider when trying to identify potential partners. As we'll discuss below, the focus of the partnership doesn't necessarily need to be interfaith engagement. Simply gathering a diverse group of participants to attend a local event or to do community service together can provide opportunities for building meaningful relationships across faith lines.

Local organizations. Moving beyond the context of colleges and universities, many local civic and religious organizations provide opportunities for interfaith engagement. Consider contacting the local Council of Churches in your area, as well as other religious and community organizations, to ask about opportunities for interfaith work. Over the years we've partnered with a wide variety of organizations, including the St. Paul Area Council of Churches (now called Interfaith Action of Greater St. Paul), the Joint Religious Legislative Coalition, and local Islamic centers.

Additionally, many civic organizations are increasingly including an interfaith component to public events. Our faculty, students, and staff have participated in several civic events that have involved representatives from a variety of faith traditions, such as an interfaith remembrance service on the tenth anniversary of 9/11 and an annual Martin Luther King Jr. march and rally.

PLANNING EVENTS

Although conversations about theological differences are important, some of the most effective events for building bridges with persons of different faiths have a separate focus. Interfaith conversations about prayer, scripture, and religious practice can help develop religious literacy about other traditions as well as helping us grow in understanding of our own traditions. In these settings, however, it can be challenging to find commonality and develop ongoing partnerships. Instead, events that focus on issues of common concern or interest allow us to cultivate meaningful relationships that help us become comfortable with navigating differences of belief and practice. While it's our experience that these sorts of events foster meaningful dialogue about significant issues, Niebuhr reminds us that "even in the midst of the most superficial of exchanges among people, there exists the possibility of someone hearing something for the first time, . . . something they come to consider of real value, to explore and build on."[7] So it's important not to underestimate the power of bringing people of different faiths together in the same space. Below we offer some suggestions for framing events in ways that promote community and partnership.

Find common interests. One of the challenges of interfaith engagement is learning to see the religious other as a fellow human being, not merely a category like "Muslim" or "Hindu" or "evangelical." Often we focus on religious labels as definitive of our identity—and the media further exacerbates this tendency. Not only does a focus on religious labels limit our ability to see a religious neighbor as a person and not just an other, it also fuels stereotypes about what "all" Muslims or Buddhists or Hindus are like. This limited focus eclipses the intersectionality of other differences (and similarities), including race, gender, and class. Just as religion is only one part of our identity as Christians (we personally are also Americans, women, liberal arts professors, mothers, and wives), we need to recognize that this is also the case for our religious neighbors.

Instead of merely highlighting theological differences, consider planning an event around shared interests. For example, take students, faculty, and staff from different religious traditions bowling, to a play, or to visit an art museum. Invite participants from different faiths to gather to discuss topics of common concern like gun violence or climate change. During such events participants can share how their faith shapes their views on these issues without becoming mired in theological differences. This allows us to recognize that shared values and common social action are possible despite participants holding different religious beliefs. Additionally, these conversations challenge stereotypes such as the false ideas that "all Muslims are violent" or that "all Christians oppose policies aimed at protecting the environment." Planning these types of events can also have a positive influence on participation rates at interfaith events, as many participants who might not initially attend an interfaith event come because of their passion for art, their concern for the environment, or their love of bowling.

Recently our campus hosted a yearlong series of interfaith events on the theme of art and faith. Each of the events was held off campus and involved Christian and Muslim students utilizing paint, spoken word, and drama as mediums for sharing personal faith stories. By focusing primarily on art and story rather than debate, religious differences were humanized and personalized. Participants encountered other persons deeply committed to living out their faith, not merely abstract religious ideas. Such experiences can help us learn how to partner together for the common good amidst religious diversity.

Serve together. Community service is another way to build bridges across faith lines by engaging participants beyond mere theological discussion. Serving others is a core value across religious traditions and has the power to unite people who believe differently around a common cause. Service allows participants from different faith traditions to spend time working together and getting to know each other in a nonthreatening context. Service also creates a venue for cultivating empathy across racial and economic lines in addition to faith lines.

For several years our campus has participated, along with several hundred other colleges and universities, in the President's Interfaith and Community Service Campus Challenge. This initiative, housed in the Office of Faith-Based and Neighborhood Partnerships and supported by the Department of Education and the Corporation for National and Community Service, seeks to utilize the power and influence of institutions of higher education to "build understanding between different communities and contribute to the common good."[8] Not only can these interfaith service events take place within a specific campus community, they can bring together participants from several different colleges and universities to serve together.

On our campus we've planned and implemented a wide variety of interfaith service events, including building and maintaining community gardens, cleaning apartments at a subsidized housing community for senior citizens, and volunteering annually at a citywide Martin Luther King Jr. Day parade and resource fair. At each of these events our Christian students, faculty, and staff have worked alongside participants from other religious traditions. Each event ends with a meal where there's a guided conversation on a religious or civic topic. For example, we've learned from local elders about building bridges across faith lines in an urban neighborhood, we've discussed Martin Luther King Jr.'s own words about interfaith engagement and service, and we've explored the role of prayer in a variety of religious traditions.

Many positive outcomes result from interfaith service. Our participants have experienced significant learning on a wide range of topics, including the problem of urban food deserts, the tensions between African Americans and African immigrants in a particular neighborhood, and the role that mosques and synagogues play in serving the communities in which they're located. On one particular occasion participants from our campus worked with Muslim and Hindu students from the University of Minnesota to clean a church property. That led our Christian campus participants to discuss with each other the need for Christians to demonstrate neighborly love by helping to clean a mosque or temple. Not only are service projects valuable because of the concrete work that's accomplished, but also because of the relationships, empathy, and spiritual growth forged in the process.

Tell stories. Although social activities and service events can help build bridges and cultivate relationships across faith lines, meaningful conversation is also essential. Remember, though, that theological debate isn't the best way to go about this. A powerful tool for accomplishing the civic and religious goals of interfaith engagement is storytelling. Stories have the power to promote common understanding and constructive partnership.

In much of his work Patel emphasizes the importance of storytelling, and in particular the content of the stories we tell, because "personal storytelling moves the encounter from competing notions of 'Truth' to varied human experiences of life, which possess the unique quality of being both infinite and common."[9] Although stories can be powerful tools for positive change, they can also be used to fuel fragmentation and fear. For example, Patel tells the story of a community of Egyptian immigrants in Jersey City, New Jersey, half of whom are Christian and half of whom are Muslim.[10] For decades Christians and Muslims in that community lived together peacefully and collaboratively, until a day in January 2005 when a family of four Egyptian Coptic Christians was brutally murdered, execution style. Before anything was known about the identity of the killers, a leader in the Christian community said, "This looks like something that Muslims would do." According to Patel, the community leader "chose to define reality for the community" in the sense that he "chose to tell a story of Muslims and Christians in perpetual and inherent conflict."

Since that day the community has remained fractured, even though the persons eventually charged with the crime weren't Muslim. Patel goes on to imagine what might have happened if, instead of defining reality in a divisive manner, the community leader had publicly said, "We as the citizens of Jersey City stand tall and proud and together as a community of pluralism against . . . extremists who might violate that effort." As Patel points out, such a positive story would have had the power to preserve community and prompt a positive response to the violence.

Patel maintains that it isn't enough that we tell stories within our own bubbles, but we must share those stories outside our bubbles as well. By building bridges between different faith communities we affirm "the identity of the constituent communities while emphasizing that the well-being of each and all depends on the health of the whole. It is the belief that the common good is best served when each community has a chance to make its unique contribution."[11]

Some sample prompts for sharing stories at bridge-building events include:

- How and why do your religious beliefs motivate you to engage in service to others?

- Who is a person from your religious tradition, historical or contemporary, that inspires you?

- Share a story of people from your own tradition, or a group of people from different faiths, who worked together for the common good. What was accomplished? Why is this significant?

- How did you come to be a follower of your religion? In what ways does this tradition give meaning to your life?

BUILDING BRIDGES THROUGH TRAVEL

An exciting aspect of interfaith engagement is taking participants to places and spaces they don't normally inhabit. Of course this can include leaving a suburban campus bubble for an urban environment; finding the intersections between religious, cultural, racial, and economic diversity in your community; and visiting different religious houses of worship. But creating interfaith engagement events can also involve taking roads less traveled.

The value of study abroad experiences for college students—as well as faculty and staff—is well-known. As we seek to broaden our understanding of the world and prepare to better navigate the challenges and opportunities of globalization, getting outside of our cultural bubbles is essential. Learning to navigate religious difference can be an important dimension of study abroad programming. Could a trip to South Africa, for example, include a study of the ways in which interfaith partnerships played a role in ending apartheid or currently play a role in addressing the HIV crisis? Might a trip to Europe include conversations with persons involved in building bridges between traditionally Christian communities and new Muslim migrants from North Africa and the Middle East? When traveling in Indonesia, India, Oman, or Northern Ireland, can participants find opportunities for discussions with religious leaders working toward religious reconciliation?

In addition to designing interfaith components to study abroad trips, we can also utilize local spaces as an accessible way to get students, faculty, and staff outside of our community bubbles. On our campus, for example, we have Sankofa trips. *Sankofa*, a term used by the Akan people of Ghana, means "It is not taboo to go back and fetch what you forgot."[12] These trips, designed as Saturday outings or spring break excursions, engage students, faculty, and staff in learning about the historical and contemporary situation of various cultural groups. Past trips have focused on the American civil rights movement, Hmong culture in the Twin Cities, and the Ojibwe and Dakota nations. On Sankofa trips, participants engage in active listening and have difficult conversations about the idea that "whatever we have been stripped of, lost, or forgotten can be reclaimed, revived, and preserved for the future."[13] And participants use their experience on the trip to engage diversity in new and constructive ways. Discussing the interactions—positive and negative—between Christians and other religious groups is an important focus of the event.

Crossing faith lines beyond our usual communities is a powerful way to develop a global view. We learn to recognize the way that culture and religion influence each other and come to understand that there's no universal way to practice a particular religion. We also "learn how to cultivate both gratitude for and critical distance from [our] cultural home,"[14] and in this way learn to balance the receptive humility and reflective commitment needed to love our religious neighbors (near and far) well.

Being a Good Guest/Host

Interfaith engagement can be a richly rewarding and perspective-changing opportunity. But it's also tricky at times. We need to be good guests and hosts so that we not only avoid offending others but also show love and respect for others despite our differing beliefs. In order to do this well, we must be willing to participate actively, openly, and sincerely. Interfaith engagement isn't academic voyeurism—being a passive spectator of someone else's life. We're not simply using others for our own intellectual fulfillment. As genuine participants we approach events and encounters with reflective commitment, imaginative empathy, and receptive humility, being willing to share, learn, and make mistakes.

Second, we must be mindful of the power dynamics at play when people from different religious and cultural traditions gather together. Whether or not we feel privileged, being a Christian is recognized by many

Interfaith engagement isn't academic voyeurism—being a passive spectator of someone else's life.

as a form of privilege in our society. Not only is religious identity itself a basis of privilege (or lack thereof), religion also intersects with class, racial and cultural background, gender, and sexuality in shaping our social standing. Interfaith events, like any civic activity, don't typically take place on a level playing field. As Omid Safi aptly describes when writing about his own experiences as a Muslim leader in interfaith engagement, "It remains absolutely and indispensably the case that the ground upon which we stand is extraordinarily differentiated. We share radically different levels of access to power, wealth, and privilege . . . and there are fundamental structural inequalities that shape the parameters in which this conversation takes place."[15] These power dynamics influence where an event is held, who's invited, who speaks, and which views are represented. Safi recounts an all-too-common experience of being taken off of a panel because his stance on a political issue differed from the stance of event sponsors. He responded to this event with the following plea:

> We have to make sure that the structures and institutions of these conversations are equally lovely and just. May it be real,

grounded, rooted, and bring them closer to God. And may we have the courage to build truthful dialogues . . . to speak from the depth of our humanity, including both the pain and suffering as well as the highest hopes for healing and reconciliation.[16]

Leveling the playing field can mean being intentional about the diversity of people participating, being equitable and just in the way resources are paid for and distributed, being sure not to rely again and again on the same marginalized group, and being sensitive to differences of belief and practice.

Here are some additional guidelines to consider when planning and implementing events that cross religious bridges:

- Prior to an event, be sure participants are aware of cultural and religious expectations regarding clothing, physical and personal space, greetings, and interaction between genders.

- Be aware of various religious dietary needs and restrictions of those who might participate.

- Utilize local community spaces and purchase food and supplies from local businesses in the area of your event as a gesture of partnership and solidarity.

- Consider the religious calendar and prayer/worship schedules of the religious groups participating when scheduling an event.

- Invite all participants who wish to do so to offer a blessing before a conversation or a meal so that all religious traditions present feel welcome.

- Remember that each participant represents only one person's way of living out a particular religious tradition. No one can speak for all Christians, all Muslims, all Hindus, and so on.

- Provide adequate opportunity for participants to engage in pre- and post-processing, as this can help ensure that the learning goals of an event are effectively met.

Additional Resources

Books and articles

+ Katie Basham and Megan Hughes, "Creating and Sustaining Interfaith Cooperation on Christian Campuses: Tools and Challenges," *Journal of College and Character* 13, no. 2 (2012): 1-7. This article describes interfaith efforts at Berea College, a Christian school with numerous religious perspectives represented on campus. It offers concrete suggestions as well as some questions that those on Christian campuses should ask in determining what interfaith efforts might look like at their institution.

+ Miriam Rosalyn Diamond, *Encountering Faith in the Classroom* (Sterling, VA: Stylus, 2008). This edited collection includes practical suggestions and theoretical discussions that emphasize the importance of creating a space in the classroom for students to "express their beliefs, dissonance, and emotions constructively . . . without fear of retribution."

+ Diana L. Eck, *Encountering God: A Journey from Bozeman to Banaras* (Boston: Beacon, 2003). Eck, director of Harvard's Pluralism Project, provides ample evidence to support the claim that interfaith dialogue is crucial in today's global society.

+ Amy Eilberg, *From Enemy to Friend: Jewish Wisdom and the Pursuit of Peace* (Maryknoll, NY: Orbis, 2014). This book draws from the author's own experience as a spiritual director and interfaith activist, classical Jewish texts, and peace and conflict theory. It provides practical and inspiring suggestions and insights into barriers to peacemaking.

+ Dana Graef, "Learning the Language of Interfaith Dialogue," *Cross-Currents* 55, no. 1 (2005): 106-20. Written from a participant's vantage point, this article provides a description of various activities of the Religious Life Council, an interfaith group at Princeton.

- Todd H. Green, *The Fear of Islam: An Introduction to Islamophobia in the West* (Minneapolis: Fortress, 2015). Green provides a useful history and context for Western anxieties about Islam, including contemporary evidence of the harm that such fear has fostered, as well as suggestions for combating Islamophobia.

- Maggie Herzig and Laura Chasin, *Fostering Dialogue Across Divides* (Watertown, MA: Public Conversations Project, 2006). This "nuts and bolts guide from the Public Conversations Project" provides numerous specific suggestions for facilitating dialogue about various "polarizing public issues." It also includes sample discussion questions and handouts.

- Ranya Idliby, Suzanne Oliver, and Priscilla Warner. *The Faith Club: A Muslim, A Christian, A Jew—Three Women Search for Understanding* (New York: Free Press, 2006). The authors describe the conversations, challenges, and rewards they experienced in their interreligious friendship. They provide concrete examples and suggestions for those who wish to engage in such dialogue.

- Victor Kazanjian and Peter Laurence, "The Journey Toward Multi-faith Community on Campus: The Religious and Spiritual Life Program at Wellesley College," *Journal of College and Character* 9, no. 2 (2007): 1-12. This article describes the theoretical basis of and goals for a campus-wide religious pluralism program at Wellesley College, a discussion particularly useful in thinking about goals that go beyond tolerance.

- Sheryl A. Kujawa-Holbrook, *God Beyond Borders: Interreligious Learning Among Faith Communities* (Eugene, OR: Pickwick, 2014). This accessible book provides both theological reflection and practical advice, such as "principles of effective interreligious practice," suggestions for sharing sacred space or planning multifaith worship services, and discussion questions to accompany each chapter.

- Robert J. Nash, DeMethra LaSha Bradley, and Arthur W. Chickering, *How to Talk About Hot Topics on Campus: From Polarization to Moral Conversation* (San Francisco: Jossey-Bass, 2008). The authors (faculty member, student affairs professional, and administrator) provide a philosophical rationale as well as many practical suggestions for promoting a culture of dialogue and conversation on campus rather than one of argument or division, even around "hot topics" such as religion and racial diversity. Particularly useful is Appendix A: A Step-by-Step How-To Guide for Facilitators and Participants When Doing Moral Conversation (by Robert J. Nash and Alissa B. Strong).

- Eboo Patel and Cassie Meyer, "The Civic Relevance of Interfaith Cooperation for Colleges and Universities," *Journal of College and Character* 12, no. 1 (2011): 1-9. The authors provide an accessible and effective overview of many issues related to interfaith cooperation: challenges we face amid religious diversity, why interfaith cooperation is so important, and what higher education might do to promote interfaith cooperation.

- Eboo Patel, *Interfaith Leadership: A Primer* (Boston: Beacon, 2016). The author, an interfaith leader and founder of Interfaith Youth Core, draws from both scholarship and experience to provide a guide to interfaith leadership, both important and practical.

- Jennifer Peace, "A Teaching Tactic for Interfaith Engagement," *Teaching Theology and Religion* 16, no. 4 (2013): 388. Peace provides step-by-step instructions for a classroom exercise in which participants tell their own story of an interfaith encounter and then listen to classmates' stories.

- Jane Idleman Smith, *Muslims, Christians, and the Challenge of Interfaith Dialogue.* (New York: Oxford University Press, 2007). The author, a Christian and specialist in Islamic Studies, provides much insight into a range of perspectives held by many Muslims on various issues related to interfaith dialogue.

TALK ABOUT IT

- Why are face-to-face encounters with people who believe differently so important?

- Which existing extracurricular activities or study abroad opportunities on your campus could be adapted to include an interfaith component?

- How might service projects and storytelling be a more effective path to interfaith engagement than theological dialogue?

GIVE IT A TRY

Make a list of possible partners in your area. Look for organizations and institutions doing interfaith work and identify the different faith traditions represented in your community.

A CHRISTIAN IN THE MUSLIM STUDENT ASSOCIATION

April Lenker, MSN, AGNP-BC, UNC Rex Cancer Center

In 2005 I was a freshman at the University of North Carolina at Chapel Hill. I immediately connected to a local church and a campus ministry, Campus Crusade for Christ. I also wanted to get plugged into a non-Christian organization. I heard of the Muslim Student Association (MSA) and was interested in learning more about Islam because most of what I knew at that point was through media.

I remember the first day walking in to MSA, one of the largest organizations on our campus. There I was met with questioning but friendly gazes. Everyone was very welcoming. Conversation quickly turned to "So why are you here?"—not in an invasive way, but out of curiosity since I was the only non-Muslim attendee. I informed them that I wanted to know more about Islam.

Since 9/11, Islam has often been present in the media. Most representations are full of violence, and stories that might portray positive aspects of Muslims are almost nonexistent. This makes it difficult to get a picture of what Islam is about. By contrast, the people I met in the MSA seemed friendly and welcoming. These Muslim students were aware of what they were up against and often felt the prejudices on campus and in the media. They were more than willing to give me an accurate portrayal of Islam.

Christianity also gets negative attention in the media. Christianity is portrayed as a Western religion full of prejudice and hypocrisy. I also wanted to bring clarity surrounding the Christian faith. I wanted to communicate and portray biblically centered Christianity.

In my first semester in MSA I learned much about Islam. I went to almost every weekly meeting and special event. The following semester I participated in a day of fasting during Ramadan and in the celebrations of Eid after Ramadan. I had several friends from Campus Crusade express interest in being involved. After talking to our director, we developed a program called "Conversation Partners," where two Muslim students were paired with two Christian students for the school year. The intention was to break down barriers and bring clarity to each faith as these conversation partners got to know each other. Over the next three years, Campus Crusade (later renamed Cornerstone) and MSA continued to participate in interfaith dialogue and events. This brought awareness and collaboration, a true model for our campus.

On a personal level, I developed close relationships with several Muslim women. Nemah was my conversation partner. We spent one afternoon each week reading from the Qur'an and the Bible. We discussed theology. She answered a lot of my questions and was extremely patient in helping me understand Islam.

I also got to know Anem and Nidah, sisters who, as I soon learned, were from my hometown. They invited me to their home for dinner and spent Thanksgiving with my family and me. We also had several conversations concerning theology and faith.

Nadiah was a student from Singapore studying abroad at UNC. Through our relationship I gained an inside view of Islam outside of the United States. I saw how Islam was woven into her culture and practices. She spent Thanksgiving with my family and we took multiple trips in my endeavor to show her every wonderful thing about North Carolina. One summer I traveled to Singapore to visit her and her family.

Ola was an active, involved leader in MSA. She was one of the first to welcome me to my first large group meeting. She was a pioneer in helping start the conversation partners and continued the interfaith events and collaboration.

During my time at UNC, being a part of MSA didn't feel like doing "interfaith work." Instead, it felt like intentionally living life with the people around me, specifically those of Islamic faith.

SOMETIMES IT TAKES ONE

Ola Mohamed, IFYC alum and fellow, immigration attorney

I cannot remember the first time I met April, but by the time I was a senior at the University of North Carolina at Chapel Hill in 2008, I knew I could count on seeing her often—not just in the student union or in class but at almost every interfaith event as well as at the weekly meetings for UNC's Muslim Students Association (MSA).

April's presence lit up the room when she entered. She had short, dark blond hair with bangs that swooshed across her forehead, blue-gray eyes, and a ready smile. What I remember most about April is her southern hospitality, genuine interest in others, love for the nursing profession, and deep devotion to her faith. April was the first evangelical Christian I came to know on a personal level, and her presence helped to nurture a broader interfaith exchange between evangelical Christians and Muslims on UNC's campus.

Around the same time I began to know April, there was a renewed effort to revitalize interfaith ties across campus faith organizations. The prominent evangelical Christian group, Campus Crusade for Christ, had recently renamed itself Cornerstone and demonstrated interest in reaching out to initiate dialogue with other student groups, among them the MSA. As the president of the MSA, I received an email correspondence from one of the Cornerstone leaders expressing the organization's desire to encourage joint events and exchange between our respective members.

I was delighted to hear of Cornerstone's outreach efforts. I was especially excited about the opportunity to open this new door of interfaith work because I had also been recently selected to serve as a fellow for the Chicago-based Interfaith Youth Core (IFYC). My goal as an IFYC fellow was to promote interfaith dialogue and community service on my campus, and especially to invite groups not traditionally invited to partake in interfaith circles.

That year (2008-2009) marked an unprecedented level of positive engagement between evangelical Christians and Muslims on UNC's campus. With active leadership and members from both the MSA and Cornerstone, the two organizations were able to host a number of events together, set up an ongoing conversation partners group, and hold one of the largest interfaith panel events in the campus's recent history. These events were not always easy. They sometimes required honest and difficult conversations. There were even some moments of tension and uncertainty. In the end, however, the overwhelming majority of the interactions were positive and eye-opening. They sparked conversations that may not have been attempted otherwise. They started friendships that may have never been fathomed.

The interfaith engagement between Muslims and evangelical Christians at UNC during my time as a student there did not necessarily flourish, however, because of the many inter-organizational emails, elaborate co-board meetings, or countless outreach meetings needed to make each interfaith idea a reality. It coalesced and grew because of the sincerity of one person—April.

Yes, Cornerstone's efforts to reach out to MSA mattered. Yes, the conversation groups and joint events mattered. However, what mattered most and what mattered first to me was April's presence. She came to MSA meetings before there were any formal efforts of exchange between the two organizations, and when she came, she listened with keen interest, she was ever respectful, and she demonstrated the best of character in all her interactions. I came to associate these attributes with April's faith. She embodied the values of evangelical Christianity in such a way that she simultaneously upheld the integrity of her faith while welcoming the faith of others.

One time April came to my apartment where we were hosting our women's weekly circle for the MSA. The topic for the evening was women's leadership in Islam. April listened attentively throughout the conversation and participated as well. I loved this about April. When she was present, she was present fully. April stayed even after the others left. We had a long conversation that evening about our goals. We shared our perspectives on careers and marriage, and how we saw our faiths woven into these life decisions.

In my mind, the personal relationship April forged with me and many of the other MSA students as a friend was the main impetus for MSA pursuing interfaith work with Cornerstone during that last year of my college experience. Her approach invited meaningful interfaith connection and encouraged the more formal events to happen. From this journey, I learned an important lesson about interfaith engagement. Sometimes it just takes one person to create a positive impression, to start a conversation, and to ultimately open a door of communication between two faiths. For UNC eight years ago, that person was April. If given the opportunity, let that person for your university, your neighborhood, or your community be you.

> **April embodied the values of Evangelical Christianity in such a way that she simultaneously upheld the integrity of her faith while welcoming the faith of others.**

Across the Bridge

In the years since we began doing interfaith work at Bethel University, it's become an increasingly urgent matter to address the challenges of religious diversity, in America as well as around the globe. Fear, ignorance, and misunderstanding are too often leading to isolationist policies, hateful speech, and even violence. One of the most dangerous forms of fear facing us today is Islamophobia.

Islamophobia—the "hatred, hostility, and fear of Islam and Muslims, and the discriminatory practices that result"—isn't new.[1] Dating back to the Middle Ages and the Crusades, the relationship between Islam and Christianity has often (though not always) been defined in terms of fear and hate. In the contemporary West, Islamophobia is fostered by stories that feature Muslims as the enemy, as a threat to democratic values and even a threat to freedom itself. These stories rely on a reductive and flawed stereotyping of Islam as "violent, antidemocratic, and misogynist."[2] Repeatedly, the news media, politicians, and films and television shows reinforce such views, rarely challenging these misguided beliefs.

The harmful consequences of Islamophobia, however, extend well beyond a limited and inaccurate understanding of Islam. The narratives that fuel this fear lead to hostile and discriminatory actions, ranging from social marginalization to hate crimes and political policies limiting the rights of Muslims. Even if we don't actively support discriminatory policies, too many American Christians follow the easy path: We retreat to our bubbles, where we can feel comfortable and secure in our own ways of perceiving the world. This does little, however, to address the problem. As with any harmful prejudice, "Islamophobia will thrive as long as those who are not its immediate victims are silent."[3]

This is why bridge-building is so important. Bridges help us build healthy civic partnerships. They foster the moral and intellectual development needed for thoughtful internal reflection about and healthy responses to religious diversity. They help us approach religious neighbors with openness instead of hostility.

College and university campuses are the ideal places to begin learning to be bridge-builders. Recently a group of our Christian students planned and hosted an event on our campus titled "Responding to Islamophobia." They hoped to get our campus community thinking and talking about how Christians could best support Muslims in our area, so they invited a panel of three Muslim speakers to share their experiences with us. The speakers represented very different walks of life: a middle-age Pakistani man who had moved to North America as a child, an African American man who finds meaning and purpose in Islam and now works with Muslim youth, and a white woman from rural Minnesota who converted from Lutheranism because of her positive friendships with Muslim graduate students from around the world. By sharing their experiences as American Muslims, they were able to humanize the issue of religious diversity for our Christian community. Those who attended the event saw and heard a bigger and more complex version of the world and of Islam than the one they typically encounter. The speakers' stories prompted fruitful discussions on issues of race, gender, and class in addition to religion. And most important they inspired us to be good neighbors by replacing fear with empathy and love.

This story reiterates the importance of Martin Buber's words that were quoted in the introduction to this book: "Certainly what one believes is important, but still more important is *how* one believes it." Imagine a world where we act on our beliefs in a spirit of receptive humility, reflective commitment, and imaginative empathy. Imagine a world where we strive for inclusion, not mere tolerance or simple affirmation. Imagine a world where the other is hospitably welcomed in love as neighbor. It's just across the bridge.

Notes

INTRODUCTION: OUT OF THE BUBBLE

[1]Eboo Patel, preface to *God Beyond Borders: Interreligious Learning Among Faith Communities*, by Sheryl A. Kujawa-Holbrook (Eugene, OR: Pickwick, 2014), x.

[2]Eboo Patel, *Acts of Faith* (Boston: Beacon Press, 2007), xv.

[3]Patel, preface to *God Beyond Borders*, xi.

[4]Nicholas M. Price, "All Nations Before God's Throne: Evangelicals in the Interfaith World," *CrossCurrents* 55, no. 3 (2005): 412.

[5]Martin Buber, *Between Man and Man*, trans. Ronald Gregor Smith (Boston: Beacon Press, 1955), 112.

[6]"Mission, Vision, and Values," Bethel University, accessed November 12, 2015, www.bethel.edu/about/mission-vision.

[7]"Our Vision," InterVarsity Christian Fellowship/USA, accessed November 12, 2015, www.intervarsity.org/about/our/our-vision.

[8]Gay L. Holcomb and Arthur J. Nonneman, "Faithful Change: Exploring and Assessing Faith Development in Christian Liberal Arts Undergraduates," *New Directions for Institutional Research* 122 (summer 2004): 100. See also Kathleen M. Goodman, "Deliberate Campus Practices to Foster Spirituality, Purpose, and Meaning," in *Spirituality in College Students' Lives*, ed. Alyssa Bryant Rockenbach and Matthew J. Mayhew (New York: Routledge, 2013), 59-60.

[9]Diana L. Eck, *Encountering God: A Spiritual Journey from Bozeman to Banaras* (Boston: Beacon Press, 2003), xvi.

[10]Warren A. Nord, *Does God Make a Difference? Taking Religion Seriously in Our Schools and Universities* (New York: Oxford University Press, 2010), 196.

[11]Alyssa N. Rockenbach et al., "Fostering the Pluralism Orientation of College Students through Interfaith Co-curricular Engagement," *Review of Higher Education* 39, no. 1 (2015): 47.

[12]Amy G. Oden, *And You Welcomed Me: A Sourcebook on Hospitality in Early Christianity* (Nashville: Abingdon, 2001), 145-47.

[13]Douglas Jacobsen and Rhonda Hustedt Jacobsen, *No Longer Invisible: Religion in University Education* (New York: Oxford University Press, 2012), 66.

[14]Buber, *Pointing the Way*, trans. Maurice Friedman (New York: Harper, 1957), 104.

1 WHY INTERFAITH ENGAGEMENT? A CIVIC IMPERATIVE

[1]Diana L. Eck, *Encountering God: A Spiritual Journey from Bozeman to Banaras* (Boston: Beacon Press, 2003), xviii.

[2]Warren A. Nord, *Does God Make A Difference? Taking Religion Seriously in Our Schools and Universities* (New York: Oxford University Press, 2010), 290.

[3]Ibid., 20, 22.

[4]Joseph Chuman, "Does Religion Cause Violence?," in *Modern Analysis of Religious Practices*, ed. Timothy R. Cullen (New York: Nova Science Publications, 2012), 81.

[5]Brian McLaren, *Why Did Jesus, Moses, the Buddha, and Mohammed Cross the Road?* (New York: Jericho Books, 2012), footnote on 38.

[6]Diana L. Eck, "Prospects for Pluralism: Voice and Vision in the Study of Religion," *Journal of the American Academy of Religion* 75, no. 4 (2007): 744.

[7]Ibid.

[8]Robert C. Spach, "Addressing the Identity-Relevance Dilemma," in *Sacred and Secular Tensions in Higher Education*, ed. Michael D. Waggoner (New York: Routledge, 2011), 187.

[9]Pavlos E. Michaelides, "Interfaith Dialogue in Global Perspective and the Necessity of Youth Involvement," *Asia-Europe Journal* 7 (2009): 449.

[10]Robert Putnam and David Campbell, *American Grace: How Religion Divides and Unites Us* (New York: Simon and Schuster, 2010), 8.

[11]Ibid., 154.

[12]Ibid., 506-7.

[13]Ibid., 520-21.

[14]Ibid., 543-44.

[15]Eboo Patel, "Religious Diversity and Cooperation on Campus," *Journal of College and Character* 9, no. 2 (2007): 5.

[16]Ibid.

[17]Pew Research Center, "Latest Trends in Religious Restrictions and Hostilities," February 26, 2015, www.pewforum.org/2015/02/26/religious-hostilities.

[18]Ibid.

[19]Ibid.

[20]Thomas Friedman, "The Real War," *New York Times*, November 27, 2001, www.nytimes.com/2001/11/27/opinion/27FRIE.html.

[21]Michaelides, "Interfaith Dialogue," 449.

[22]Ron Kronish, "Interreligious Dialogue in the Service of Peace," *CrossCurrents* 58, no. 2 (2008): 225.

[23]Robert Wuthnow, *America and the Challenges of Religious Diversity* (Princeton, NJ: Princeton University Press, 2005), 78.

[24]Ibid., 89.

[25]Martha Nussbaum, *The New Religious Intolerance* (Cambridge, MA: Harvard University Press, 2012), 2.

[26]Jacob Stutzman, "Christian Privilege in American Political Discourse: Two Case Studies," paper presented at the National Communication Association National Convention, Religious Communication Association, Rhetorical Studies Division, San Diego, CA, 2007.

[27]Nussbaum, *New Religious Intolerance*, 2.

[28]Ibid., 9.

[29]"President Barack Obama's Inaugural Address," the White House blog, January 21, 2009, www.whitehouse.gov/blog/2009/01/21/president-barack-obamas-inaugural-address.

[30]Putnam and Campbell, *American Grace*, 497.

[31]Miroslav Volf, *A Public Faith: How Followers of Christ Should Serve the Common Good* (Grand Rapids: Brazos, 2011), x.

[32]Gustav Niebuhr, *Beyond Tolerance: Searching for Interfaith Understanding in America* (New York: Viking, 2008), xx.

[33]Robert D. Putnam, "*E Pluribus Unum*: Diversity and Community in the Twenty-first Century. The 2006 Johan Skytte Prize Lecture," *Scandinavian Political Studies* 30, no. 2 (2007): 139.

[34]Patel, *Acts of Faith*, xv.

188   *Notes to Pages 25-30*

[35]Eboo Patel, *Sacred Ground: Pluralism, Prejudice, and the Promise of America* (Boston: Beacon Press, 2012), 71.

[36]Abraham Joshua Heschel, "No Religion Is an Island," in *No Religion Is an Island: Abraham Joshua Heschel and Interreligious Dialogue*, ed. Harold Kasimow and Byron L. Sherwin (Maryknoll, NY: Orbis Books, 1991), 7.

[37]Wuthnow, *America and the Challenges*, 294.

[38]Eck, *Encountering God*, xi.

[39]Diana L. Eck, "American Religious Pluralism: Civic and Theological Discourse," in *Democracy and the New Religious Pluralism*, ed. Thomas Banchoff (New York: Oxford University Press, 2007), 252.

[40]Adam C. LaMonica, "The *Humanist* Interview with Eboo Patel," *Humanist* (May-June 2009): 31.

[41]Miroslav Volf, *Allah: A Christian Response* (New York: HarperOne, 2011), 13.

[42]Ibid.

[43]Ibid., 218.

[44]Kristin Johnson Largen, *Finding God Among Our Neighbors* (Minneapolis: Fortress, 2013), 218.

[45]Volf, *Allah*, 13-14.

[46]"An Introduction," Evangelical Manifesto, March 9, 2016, www.evangelical manifesto.com.

[47]"An Evangelical Manifesto: A Declaration of Evangelical Identity and Public Commitment," Evangelical Manifesto, May 7, 2008, www.evangelical manifesto.com/wp-content/uploads/2016/03/Evangelical_Manifesto.pdf.

[48]Nussbaum, *New Religious Intolerance*, 23.

[49]Ibid., 58.

[50]Robert D. Putnam, *Bowling Alone* (New York: Simon and Schuster, 2000), 363.

[51]Putnam, "*E Pluribus Unum*," 138.

[52]Ibid., 140.

[53]Ibid., 148.

[54]Ibid., 149.

[55]Ibid., 159.

[56]Putnam and Campbell, *American Grace*, 493.

[57]Putnam, *Bowling Alone*, 137.

[58]Ashutosh Varshney, *Ethnic Conflict and Civic Life* (New Haven, CT: Yale University Press, 2002), 5-6.

59Ibid., 9.

60Simon Mary Asese Aihiokhai, "'Love One Another As I Have Loved You': The Place of Friendship in Interfaith Dialogue," *Journal of Ecumenical Studies* 48, no. 4 (2013): 493.

61Putnam, *Bowling Alone*, 363.

62Ibid., 493.

63Ibid.

64"Wingspread Declaration on Religion and Public Life: Engaging Higher Education," The Society for Values in Higher Education, Accessed April 2, 2015, www.svhe.org/PDFS/WingspreadDeclarationTextformat.pdf.

65Ibid.

66Nord, *Does God Make a Difference*, 141.

67Patel, *Sacred Ground*, 121.

68Ibid., 95-96.

69Ibid., 118.

70Niebuhr, *Beyond Tolerance*, 34.

71Eck, "American Religious Pluralism," 252.

72Ibid., 253.

73Patel, *Sacred Ground*, 69.

74Niebuhr, *Beyond Tolerance*, 35.

75Patel, *Sacred Ground*, 140.

76Ibid.

2 Why Interfaith Engagement? A Religious Imperative

1Eboo Patel, *Sacred Ground: Pluralism, Prejudice, and the Promise of America* (Boston: Beacon Press: 2012), 46.

2Ibid.

3Brian D. McLaren, "Entering without Knocking," in *My Neighbor's Faith*, eds. Jennifer Howe Peace, Or N. Rose, and Gregory Mobley (Maryknoll, NY: Orbis, 2012), 5.

4Søren Kierkegaard, *Works of Love*, trans. Howard and Edna Hong (New York: Harper and Brothers, 1926), 36.

5Ibid., 38.

6Ibid., 158.

7Ibid., 97.

8Ibid., 75.

9Ibid., 53.

[10]Amy G. Oden, *And You Welcomed Me: A Sourcebook on Hospitality in Early Christianity* (Nashville: Abingdon, 2001), 146.

[11]Ibid.

[12]Ibid.

[13]Ibid., 147.

[14]Craig Dykstra, *Growing in the Life of Faith: Education and Christian Practices* (Louisville: Geneva, 1999), 60.

[15]John Koenig, *New Testament Hospitality: Partnership with Strangers as Promise and Mission* (Philadelphia: Fortress, 1985), 126.

[16]Dykstra, *Growing in the Life of Faith*, 77.

[17]Oden, *And You Welcomed Me*, 50.

[18]Ibid.

[19]Ibid.

[20]Linda J. Vogel, *Teaching and Learning in Communities of Faith* (San Francisco: Jossey-Bass, 1991), 108.

[21]David I. Smith and Barbara Carvill, *The Gift of the Stranger: Faith, Hospitality, and Language Learning* (Grand Rapids: Eerdmans, 2000), 91.

[22]Oden, *And You Welcomed Me*, 14.

[23]Anthony J. Gittins, *Gifts and Strangers: Meeting the Challenge of Inculturation* (New York: Paulist, 1989), xi.

[24]Oden, *And You Welcomed Me*, 36.

[25]Gittins, *Gifts and Strangers*, 105.

[26]Oden, *And You Welcomed Me*, 147.

[27]Patel, *Sacred Ground*, 91.

[28]Ibid.

[29]Dana Graef, "Learning the Language of Interfaith Dialogue," *CrossCurrents* 55, no. 1 (2005): 118.

[30]Michele Hershberger, *A Christian View of Hospitality: Expecting Surprises* (Scottdale, PA: Herald, 1999), 62.

[31]Ibid., 166.

[32]Elizabeth Newman, "Hospitality and Christian Higher Education," *Christian Scholar's Review* 33, no. 1 (2003): 87.

[33]Livingstone A. Thompson, *A Formula for Conversation: Christians and Muslims in Dialogue* (Lanham, MD: University Press of America, 2007), 67.

[34]Ibid., 68.

[35]Volker Kuster, "Toward an Intercultural Theology: Paradigm Shifts in Missiology, Ecumenics, and Comparative Religion," in *Theology and the*

Religions: A Dialogue, ed. Viggo Mortenson (Grand Rapids: Eerdmans, 2003), 179.

[36]Marion H. Larson and Sara L. H. Shady, "Love My (Religious) Neighbor: A Pietist Approach to Christian Responsibility in a Pluralistic World," in *The Pietist Vision of Christian Higher Education*, ed. Christopher Gehrz (Downers Grove, IL: IVP Academic, 2015), 140.

[37]Thompson, *A Formula for Conversation*, 21.

[38]Ibid.

[39]Martin E. Marty, *When Faiths Collide* (Malden, MA: Blackwell, 2005), 129.

[40]Miroslav Volf, *Allah: A Christian Response* (New York: HarperOne, 2011), 207.

[41]Caroline Westerhoff, *Good Fences: The Boundaries of Hospitality* (Harrisburg, PA: Morehouse, 1999), 49.

[42]Mireille Rosello, *Postcolonial Hospitality: The Immigrant as Guest* (Stanford, CA: Stanford University Press, 2001), 172, 175.

[43]Miroslav Volf, *A Public Faith: How Followers of Christ Should Serve the Common Good* (Grand Rapids: Brazos, 2011), 109.

[44]Ibid.

[45]Oden, *And You Welcomed Me*, 15.

[46]Volf, *Allah*, 203.

[47]Larson and Shady, "Love My (Religious) Neighbor," 142.

[48]Lee C. Camp, *Who is My Enemy? Questions American Christians Must Face about Islam—and Themselves* (Grand Rapids: Brazos, 2011).

[49]Todd H. Green, *The Fear of Islam: An Introduction to Islamophobia in the West* (Minneapolis: Fortress, 2015), 268.

[50]Douglas Pratt, "Christian Discipleship and Interfaith Engagement," *Pacifica* 22 (October 2009): 321.

[51]Volf, *Allah*, 205, 261.

[52]"Christian Witness in a Multi-Religious World: Recommendations for Conduct," *The Ecumenical Review* 63, no. 3 (2011): 351-52.

[53]Ibid., 349-51.

[54]Volf, *Allah*, 211.

[55]Ibid., 212.

[56]Ibid., 207.

[57]Brian D. McLaren, *Why Did Jesus, Moses, the Buddha, and Mohammed Cross the Road? Christian Identity in a Multi-faith World* (New York: Jericho Books, 2012), 262.

⁵⁸Rowan Williams, "A Common Word for the Common Good," Dr Rowan
Williams: Archbishop of Canterbury, July 14, 2008, rowanwilliams
.archbishopofcanterbury.org/articles.php/1107/a-common-word-for-the
-common-good.

⁵⁹Ibid.

3 Aren't We Better Off in the Bubble?
Remedies from Two Parables

¹Brian McLaren, *Why Did Jesus, Moses, the Buddha, and Mohammed
Cross the Road?* (New York: Jericho Books, 2012), 15.

²Eboo Patel, *Sacred Ground: Pluralism, Prejudice, and the Promise of
America* (Boston: Beacon Press, 2012), 142.

³Mark Labberton, *The Dangerous Act of Loving Your Neighbor* (Downers
Grove, IL: InterVarsity Press, 2010), 47, 50.

⁴McLaren, *Why Did Jesus*, 69.

⁵Ibid., 43.

⁶Ibid., 20.

⁷Ibid., 41.

⁸Ibid., 43.

⁹Ibid., 42.

¹⁰Warren J. Blumenfeld, "Christian Privilege and the Promotion of 'Secular'
and Not-So 'Secular' Mainline Christianity in Public Schooling and the
Larger Society," *Equity and Excellence in Education* 39, no. 3 (2006): 195.

¹¹Ibid., 199.

¹²Ellen E. Fairchild, "Christian Privilege, History, and Trends in U. S. Religion," *New Directions for Student Services* 125 (spring 2009): 5.

¹³Wuthnow, *America and the Challenges of Religious Diversity* (Princeton,
NJ: Princeton University Press, 2005), 169.

¹⁴Jason Wiedel, *Persecution Complex: Why American Christians Need to
Stop Playing the Victim* (Edmond, OK: CrowdScribed, 2014), 46.

¹⁵Christian Smith, *Christian America? What Evangelicals Really Want*
(Berkeley, CA: University of California Press, 2000), 70.

¹⁶Ibid., 4.

¹⁷Nicholas M. Price, "All Nations Before God's Throne: Evangelicals in the
Interfaith World," *CrossCurrents* 55, no. 3 (2005): 405.

¹⁸Warren J. Blumenfeld and Kathryn Jaekel, "Exploring Levels of Christian
Privilege Awareness among Preservice Teachers," *Journal of Social Issues*
68, no. 1 (2012): 143.

[19]Matthew J. Mayhew, Nicholas A. Bowman, and Alyssa Bryant Rockenbach, "Silencing Whom? Linking Campus Climates for Religious, Spiritual, and Worldview Diversity to Student Worldviews," *Journal of Higher Education* 85, no. 2 (2014): 222.

[20]Nicholas A. Bowman and Jenny L. Small, "Do College Students Who Identify with a Privileged Religion Experience Greater Spiritual Development? Exploring Individual and Institutional Dynamics," *Research in Higher Education* 51 (2010): 598.

[21]Alyssa N. Bryant, "Evangelicals on Campus: An Exploration of Culture, Faith, and College Life," in *Sacred and Secular Tensions in Higher Education*, ed. Michael D. Waggoner (New York: Routledge, 2011), 126.

[22]Mayhew et. al., "Silencing Whom?," 222.

[23]Sheryl A. Kujawa-Holbrook, *God Beyond Borders: Interreligious Learning Among Faith Communities* (Eugene, OR: Pickwick, 2014), xxvii.

[24]Ibid., xxviii.

[25]McLaren, *Why Did Jesus*, 63.

[26]Ibid., 83-84.

[27]Carl. E. Braaten, "The Christian Faith in an Inter-Faith Context," *Dialog: A Journal of Theology* 43, no. 3 (2004): 236.

[28]Christian Smith, *American Evangelicalism: Embattled and Thriving* (Chicago: University of Chicago Press), 121.

[29]Thomas W. Ogletree, *Hospitality to the Stranger: Dimensions of Moral Understanding* (Philadelphia: Fortress, 1985), 119-20.

[30]McLaren, *Why Did Jesus*, 84.

[31]See, for example, Robert Putnam, *Bowling Alone* (New York: Simon and Schuster, 2001).

[32]Bob Zurinsky, "The Story We Share," *Christian Century* 123, no. 4 (2015), 22.

[33]McLaren, *Why Did Jesus*, 63.

[34]Amy-Jill Levine, *Short Stories by Jesus: The Enigmatic Parables of a Controversial Rabbi* (New York: HarperOne, 2014), 25.

[35]McLaren, *Why Did Jesus*, 162.

[36]Ibid.

[37]McLaren, *Why Did Jesus*, 163.

[38]Levine, *Short Stories by Jesus*, 96.

[39]Patel, *Sacred Ground*, 144.

[40]David I. Smith, *Learning from the Stranger* (Grand Rapids: Eerdmans, 2009), 75.

⁴¹Jeannine Hill Fletcher, *Motherhood as Metaphor: Engendering Interreligious Dialogue* (NY: Fordham, 2013), 202.

⁴²Joshua Graves, *How Not to Kill a Muslim* (Eugene, OR: Cascade, 2015), 29.

⁴³Ibid., 39.

⁴⁴Ibid., 41.

⁴⁵Mark W. Thomsen, "Expanding the Scope of God's Grace: Christian Perspectives and Values for Interfaith Relations," *Currents in Theology and Mission* 40.2 (April 2013): 90.

⁴⁶Levine, *Stories by Jesus*, 105.

4 A MODEL FOR INTERFAITH ENGAGEMENT

¹Portions of this chapter were previously published in the following articles: Sara L. H. Shady and Marion H. Larson, "Tolerance, Empathy, or Inclusion? Insights from Martin Buber," *Educational Theory* 60, no. 1 (2010): 81-96, and Marion H. Larson and Sara L. H. Shady, "Interfaith Dialogue in a Pluralistic World: Insights from Martin Buber and Miroslav Volf," *Journal of College and Character* 10, no. 3 (2009): 1-9.

²The model of inclusion we describe and support is *not* the same as John Hick's inclusivist model regarding the theological status of other religions. We are focusing on a model for healthy interfaith dialogue and cooperation in a *civic* sense, not making a theological argument. We believe theological inclusivists, exclusivists, and pluralists are all capable of adopting our model of inclusion within the context of interfaith engagement.

³Martin Buber, *Between Man and Man*, trans. Ronald Gregor Smith (Boston: Beacon Press, 1955), 19.

⁴Martin Buber, *Pointing the Way*, trans. Maurice Friedman (New York: Harper, 1957), 102.

⁵Martin Buber, *I and Thou*, trans. Ronald Gregor Smith (New York: Charles Scribner's Sons, 1958). We have chosen to quote from and utilize the language of Smith's translation throughout this book. An alternative translation, which translates "Ich und Du" as "I and You" is also available. See Martin Buber, *I and Thou*, trans. Walter Kaufmann (New York: Simon and Schuster, 1970).

⁶Buber, *Between Man and Man*, 97.

⁷Ibid., 99.

⁸Buber, *I and Thou*, 11.

[9] Miroslav Volf, *Exclusion and Embrace: A Theological Exploration of Identity, Otherness, and Reconciliation* (Nashville: Abingdon Press, 1996), 91.

[10] Ibid., 66.

[11] Miroslav Volf, "A Vision of Embrace: Theological Perspectives on Cultural Identity and Conflict," *Ecumenical Review* 47 (1995): 199.

[12] Steven Kepnes, *The Text as Thou: Martin Buber's Dialogical Hermeneutics and Narrative Theology* (Bloomington, IN: Indiana University Press, 1992), 24, 59, 72.

[13] Ibid., 31.

[14] Volf, *Exclusion and Embrace*, 141.

[15] Ibid., 203.

[16] Ibid., 141.

[17] Ibid., 147.

[18] Volf, "A Vision of Embrace," 203.

[19] Volf, *Exclusion and Embrace*, 145.

[20] Volf, "Living," 10.

[21] Volf, *Exclusion and Embrace*, 251.

[22] Ibid.

[23] Miroslav Volf, "In My Own Voice? A Man Relates the Effect of Christianity on His Life," *Christian Century*, December 15, 1999, 1234.

[24] Volf, "Your Scripture," 43.

[25] Volf, "Living," 19.

[26] Volf, *Exclusion and Embrace*, 252.

[27] Miroslav Volf, "Be Particular. Faith Matters. Interfaith Dialogue," *Christian Century*, January 25, 2003, 33.

[28] Quoted in Kepnes, *Text as Thou*, 149.

[29] Volf, "Living," 9.

[30] Martin Buber, *Pointing the Way*, trans. Maurice Friedman (New York: Harper and Row, 1963), 102.

[31] Buber, "The Land and Its Possessors," in *Israel and the World* (New York: Schocken Books, 1963), 213.

[32] Buber, *Pointing the Way*, 103.

[33] For some introductory reading on this topic, consider Robert Audi and Nicholas Wolterstorff, *Religion in the Public Sphere: the Place of Religious Convictions in Political Debate* (Lanham, MD: Rowman & Littlefield Publishers, 1997).

[34]Richard Rorty, "Religion in the Public Square: A Reconsideration," *Journal of Religious Ethics* 31, no. 1 (2003): 141. Note that in this article, Rorty actually softens his historical position somewhat in light of having considered the work of Nicholas Wolterstorff on the topic. The softened version, however, still promotes secular neutrality as the best approach.

[35]Martin Buber, "Autobiographical Fragments," in *The Philosophy of Martin Buber*, ed. Paul Arthur Schlipp and Maurice Friedman (LaSalle, IL: Open Court Publishing, 1967), 8.

[36]Buber, *Between Man and Man*, 18-19.

[37]Victor Kazanjian and Peter Laurence, "The Journey Toward Multi-faith Community on Campus: The Religious and Spiritual Life Program at Wellesley College," *Journal of College and Character* 9, no. 2 (2007), 5.

[38]Paul Mendes-Flohr, "Reflections on the Promise and Limitations of Interfaith Dialogue," *European Judaism* 46, no. 1 (2013): 7.

[39]Kepnes, *Text as Thou*, 131.

[40]Robert Gibbs, "Reading with Others: Levinas' Ethics and Scriptural Reasoning," in *The Promise of Scriptural Reasoning*, ed. David C. Ford and C. C. Pecknold (Oxford, UK: Blackwell, 2006), 175.

[41]Emmanuel Levinas, "Martin Buber and the Theory of Knowledge," in *The Levinas Reader*, ed. Sean Hand (Oxford, UK: Blackwell, 1989), 67.

[42]Martin Buber, "Replies to My Critics," in *The Philosophy of Martin Buber*, ed. Paul Arthur Schilpp (La Salle, IL: Open Court, 1967), 723.

[43]Gibbs, "Reading with Others," 175.

[44]Ryan C. Urbano, "Levinas and Interfaith Dialogue," *Heythrop Journal* 53, no. 1 (2012): 153.

[45]Paul F. Knitter, "Is the Pluralist Model a Western Imposition? A Response in Five Voices," in *The Myth of Religious Superiority*, ed. Paul F. Knitter (Mayknoll, NY: Orbis Books, 2005), 40.

[46]Ibid., 38.

[47]There is a lengthy, and much commented on, conversation between Levinas and Buber on the issue of asymmetry versus reciprocity. For an introduction to this debate, see Emmanuel Levinas, "Martin Buber and the Theory of Knoweldge," in *The Philosophy of Martin Buber*, ed. Paul Arthur Schilpp (La Salle, IL: Open Court, 1967), 133-50, and Martin Buber, "Replies to My Critics."

[48]Omid Safi, "The Asymmetry of Interfaith Dialogue," *On Being*, October

29, 2015, onbeing.org/blog/omid-safi-the-asymmetry-of-interfaith
-dialogue/8076.

[49]Ibid.

[50]Martin Marty, *When Faiths Collide* (Oxford, UK: Wiley Blackwell, 2004),
146.

5 CULTIVATING VIRTUES FOR INTERFAITH ENGAGEMENT

[1]Gustav Niebuhr, *Beyond Tolerance* (New York: Viking), xxiv.

[2]This chapter contains portions published earlier in Marion H. Larson
and Anna Wilson, "Room at the Table: Cornille and the Possibility for
Religious Dialogue," *Journal of College and Character* 11, no. 1 (2010):
1-10, and Marion H. Larson and Sara L. H. Shady, "Cultivating Student
Learning Across Faith Lines," *Liberal Education* (summer 2013):
44-51.

[3]Catherine Cornille, *The Im-Possibility of Interreligious Dialogue* (New
York: Herder and Herder, 2008), 71. ·

[4]See Martha Nussbaum, *Cultivating Humanity: A Classical Defense of
Reform in Liberal Education* (Cambridge, MA: Harvard University Press,
1998), and *The New Religious Intolerance: Overcoming the Politics of Fear
in an Anxious Age* (Cambridge, MA: Belknap Press, 2012).

[5]Nussbaum, *New Religious Intolerance*, 99-100.

[6]Ibid., 140.

[7]Amy Eilberg, *From Enemy to Friend: Jewish Wisdom and the Pursuit of
Peace* (Maryknoll, NY: Orbis, 2014), 56.

[8]Cornille, *Im-Possibility*, 10.

[9]Niebuhr, *Beyond Tolerance*, xxxvi.

[10]Larson and Wilson, "Room at the Table," 8.

[11]Cornille, *Im-Possibility*, 22.

[12]Eilberg, *From Enemy to Friend*, 247.

[13]Cornille, *Im-Possibility*, 60.

[14]Ibid., 71-72.

[15]Ibid., 79.

[16]Larson and Wilson, "Room at the Table," 5.

[17]Robert Wuthnow, *America and the Challenges of Religious Diversity*
(Princeton, NJ: Princeton University Press, 2007), 311-12.

[18]Eboo Patel, "Religious Diversity and Cooperation on Campus," *Journal of
College and Character* 9, no. 1 (2007): 7.

[19]Miriam McCormick, "Responsible Believing," in *Toward a Pedagogy of Belief and Doubt*, Teagle Foundation White Paper, ed. Sydney Watts (University of Richmond, 2008), 32.

[20]Ibid., 38.

[21]Larson and Wilson, "Room at the Table," 5.

[22]Ibid.

[23]Nussbaum, *Cultivating Humanity*, 9.

[24]Larson and Wilson, "Room at the Table," 6.

[25]Cornille, *Im-Possibility*, 138.

[26]Ibid., 153.

[27]Larson and Wilson, "Room at the Table," 7.

[28]Ibid.

[29]Nussbaum, *Cultivating Humanity*, 11.

[30]Ibid., 85.

[31]Cornille, *Im-Possibility*, 95.

[32]Ibid., 111.

[33]Larson and Wilson, "Room at the Table," 6.

[34]Robert J. Nash and DeMethra LaSha Bradley, "The Different Spiritualities of the Students We Teach," in *The American University in a Postsecular Age*, ed. Douglas Jacobsen and Rhonda Hustedt Jacobsen (New York: Oxford University Press, 2008), 135.

[35]Larson and Wilson, "Room at the Table," 6.

[36]Ibid.

[37]Nussbaum, *New Religious Intolerance*, 144.

[38]Ibid., 118-19.

[39]Ibid., 146.

[40]Nussbaum, *Cultivating Humanity*, 259.

[41]Ranya Idliby, Suzanne Oliver, and Priscilla Warner, *The Faith Club: A Muslim, A Christian, and A Jew—Three Women Search for Understanding* (New York: Free Press, 2006), 256.

[42]Eilberg, *From Enemy to Friend*, 79.

[43]Cornille, *Im-Possibility*, 291.

6 INSIDE THE BUBBLE: CREATING A NURTURING LEARNING ENVIRONMENT

[1]John D. Lottes, "Toward a Christian Theology of Hospitality to Other Religions on Campus," *Currents in Theology and Mission* 31, no. 1 (2005): 27.

²Gay L. Holcomb and Arthur J. Nonneman, "Faithful Change: Exploring and Assessing Faith Development in Christian Liberal Arts Undergraduates," *New Directions for Institutional Research* 122 (summer 2004): 94.

³Matthew J. Mayhew and Alyssa N. Bryant, "Achievement or Arrest? The Influence of the Collegiate Religious and Spiritual Climate on Students' Worldview Commitment," *Research in Higher Education* 54, no. 1 (2013): 64.

⁴Alyssa Bryant Rockenbach and Matthew J. Mayhew, "How the College Religious and Spiritual Climate Shapes Students' Ecumenical Orientation," *Research in Higher Education* 54, no. 4 (2013): 462.

⁵Alyssa Bryant Rockenbach and Matthew J. Mayhew, "How Institutional Contexts and College Experiences Shape Ecumenical Worldview Development," in *Spirituality in College Students' Lives*, ed. Alyssa Bryant Rockenbach and Matthew J. Mayhew (New York: Routledge, 2013), 90.

⁶Ibid.

⁷Ibid.

⁸Robert J. Nash, *Spirituality, Ethics, Religion, and Teaching: A Professor's Journey* (New York: Peter Lang, 2002), 175.

⁹Jane Idleman Smith, *Muslims, Christians, and the Challenge of Interfaith Dialogue* (New York: Oxford University Press, 2007), 122.

¹⁰Charles Soukup and James Keaten, "Humanizing and Dehumanizing Responses Across Four Orientations to Religious Otherness," in *A Communication Perspective on Interfaith Dialogue*, ed. Daniel S. Brown Jr. (Lanham, MD: Lexington Books, 2013), 49.

¹¹Soukup and Keaten, "Humanizing and Dehumanizing," 51.

¹²Ibid.

¹³Ibid., 49-50.

¹⁴Robert Wuthnow, *America and the Challenges of Religious Diversity* (Princeton, NJ: Princeton University Press, 2007), 312.

¹⁵W. T. Dickens, "Frank Conversations: Promoting Peace Among the Abrahamic Traditions Through Interreligious Dialogue," *Journal of Religious Ethics* 34, no. 3 (2006): 407, 416.

¹⁶Ibid., 416-17.

¹⁷Tony Richie, "Approaching the Problem of Religious Truth in a Pluralistic World: A Pentecostal-Charismatic Contribution," *Journal of Ecumenical Studies* 43, no. 3 (2008): 356.

¹⁸P. Jesse Rine, "Christian College Persistence in the Postmodern Turn," in *Spirituality in College Students' Lives*, 70. See also Richie, "Approaching," 356.

[19]Mikael Stenmark, "Exclusivism, Tolerance, and Interreligious Dialogue," *Studies in Interreligious Dialogue* 16 (2006): 109.

[20]Wuthnow, *America and the Challenges,* 104.

[21]Robert Putnam, *Bowling Alone: The Collapse and Revival of American Community* (New York: Simon and Schuster, 2000), 135.

[22]An exception to this would be an event where participants will be together only one time. Inclusion is something that's practiced over time in ongoing relationships. Tolerance or affirmation may be the healthiest approaches to take in short-term interactions.

[23]Adir Cohen, "Martin Buber and Changes in Modern Education," *Oxford Review of Education* 5, no. 1 (1979): 90.

[24]For example, see John Bennett, *Academic Life: Hospitality, Ethics, and Spirituality* (Bolton, MA: Anker, 2003), 47, and Steven Kepnes, *Text as Thou* (Bloomington, IN: Indiana University Press, 1992), 149.

[25]The issue of trust is further explored by Martin Buber in *Between Man and Man,* trans. Ronald Gregor Smith (Boston: Beacon Press, 1955), 106-7. See also Charles V. Willie, "Confidence, Trust, and Respect: The Preeminent Goals of Educational Reform," *The Journal of Negro Education* 69, no. 4 (2000): 259, and John Thompson, "'The Between' of Teaching Sociology: Ways of Knowing and Teaching," *Teaching Sociology* 24, no. 3 (1996): 322.

[26]Martin Buber, *Pointing the Way,* trans. Maurice Friedman (New York: Harper, 1957), 105.

[27]Stephen D. Brookfield and Mary E. Hess, "How Can We Teach Authentically? Reflective Practice in the Dialogical Classroom," in *Teaching Reflectively in Theological Contexts: Promises and Contradictions,* ed. Mary E. Hess and Stephen D. Brookfield (Malabar, FL: Krieger Publishing, 2008), 12-13.

[28]Matthew L. Skinner, "How Can Students Learn to Trust Us as We Challenge Who They Are? Building Trust and Trustworthiness in a Biblical Studies Classroom," in *Teaching Reflectively,* 105.

[29]Ibid., 105-6.

[30]Dona Warren, "Philosophy and Religious Disagreements in the Classroom," in *Encountering Faith in the Classroom,* ed. Miriam Rosalyn Diamond (Sterling, VA: Stylus, 2008), 137.

[31]Martin Buber, *Between Man and Man,* 104.

[32]Linda J. Vogel, *Teaching and Learning in Communities of Faith* (San Francisco: Jossey-Bass, 1991), 104, 108.

[33]Peggy Catron, "Blinking in the Sunlight: Exploring the Fundamentalist Perspective," in *Encountering Faith in the Classroom*, 72.

[34]Mano Singham, "When Faith and Science Collide," in *Encountering Faith in the Classroom*, 153.

[35]Robert J. Nash, DeMethra LaSha Bradley, and Arthur W. Chickering, *How to Talk About Hot Topics on Campus: From Polarization to Moral Conversation* (San Francisco: Jossey-Bass, 2008), 20.

[36]Ibid., 21-22.

[37]Robert J. Nash and Sue M. Baskette, "Teaching About Religious and Spiritual Pluralism in a Professional Education Course," in Diamond, *Encountering Faith in the Classroom*, 195.

[38]Ibid., 196.

[39]Brookfield and Hess, "How Can We Teach Authentically?," 11.

[40]Skinner, "How Can Students Learn to Trust," 109.

[41]Barbara S. Stengal, "The Complex Case of Fear and Safe Space," *Studies in Philosophy and Education* 29, no. 6 (2010): 539.

[42]Jenny L. Small, *Understanding College Students' Spiritual Identities: Different Faiths, Varied Worldviews* (New York: Hampton Press, 2011), 140.

[43]Ibid.

[44]Stephen D. Brookfield, *The Skillful Teacher*, 2nd ed. (San Francisco: Jossey-Bass, 2006), 75.

[45]Ibid., 84.

[46]Ibid., 93.

[47]Skinner, "How Can Students Learn to Trust," 111.

[48]Small, *Understanding College Students' Spiritual Identities*, 140.

[49]Ibid., 141. Similar conclusions are reached in the research conducted by Matthew J. Mayhew, Nicolas A. Bowman, and Alyssa Bryant Rockenbach. See, for example, "Silencing Whom? Linking Campus Climates for Religious, Spiritual, and Worldview Diversity to Student Worldviews," *Journal of Higher Education* 85, no. 2 (2014): 219-45.

[50]Small, *Understanding College Students' Spiritual Identities*, 147.

[51]S. Alan Ray, "Interfaith Dialogue and Higher Education," *Liberal Education* 96, no. 3 (2010): 42.

[52]Ibid.

[53]Ibid.

[54]Ibid.

[55]Small, *Understanding College Students' Spiritual Identities,* 147.

[56]Ibid., 148.

[57]Reina C. Neufeldt, "Interfaith Dialogue: Assessing Theories of Change," *Peace and Change* 36, no. 3 (2011): 359.

7 Inside the Bubble: Sample Learning Activities

[1]Parker Palmer, "Community, Conflict, and Ways of Knowing: Ways to Deepen Our Educational Agenda," Center for Courage and Renewal, 2006, www.couragerenewal.org/?q=resources/writings/community.

[2]Parker Palmer, *To Know As We Are Known: A Spirituality of Education* (New York: Harper and Row, 1983), 91.

[3]Palmer, "Community, Conflict, and Ways of Knowing."

[4]See, for example, Robert J. Nash, "'Facing One Another in This Place': Using Moral Conversation to Talk About Controversial Topics in College Settings," *Journal of College and Character* 9, no. 4 (April 2008): 5-6; Palmer, *To Know as We Are Known,* 91-100; and www.ifyc.org.

[5]William E. Powell, "On Creating a Space: An Interview with Parker Palmer," *Families in Society* 82, no. 1 (2001): 20.

[6]Ibid.

[7]Peter Elbow, "The Believing Game," in *Nurturing the Peacemakers in Our Students,* ed. Chris Weber (Portsmouth, NH: Heinemann, 2006), 18-19.

[8]Peter Elbow, "The Believing Game or Methodological Believing," *JAEPL* 14 (Winter 2008-9): 3.

[9]Elbow, "The Believing Game or Methodological Believing," 1.

[10]Ibid., 4.

[11]Ibid., 2.

[12]Ibid., 4.

[13]Ibid., 5-6.

[14]Peter Elbow, "Bringing the Rhetoric of Assent and the Believing Game Together—and into the Classroom," *College English* 67, no. 4 (2005): 390.

[15]Elbow, "The Believing Game or Methodological Believing," 7.

[16]Ibid., 8.

[17]Elbow, "Bringing the Rhetoric of Assent," 394.

[18]Ibid., 395.

[19]Marsha Lee Baker, Eric Dieter, and Zachary Dobbins, "The Art of Being Persuaded: Wayne Booth's Mutual Inquiry and the Trust to Listen," *Composition Studies* 42, no. 1 (2014): 22.

[20]Elbow, "Bringing the Rhetoric of Assent," 395.

[21]Ibid.

[22]Baker, Dieter, and Dobbins, "The Art of Being Persuaded," 14.

[23]Ibid., 21-22.

[24]Ibid., 22.

[25]Martha Nussbaum, *Cultivating Humanity: A Classical Defense of Reform in Liberal Education* (Cambridge, MA: Harvard University Press, 1998), 100.

[26]Robert Kunzman, "Imaginative Engagement with Religious Diversity in Public School Classrooms," *Religious Education* 101, no. 4 (2006), 520.

[27]Nussbaum, *Cultivating Humanity*, 11.

[28]John Paul Lederach, "The Moral Imagination: The Art and Soul of Building Peace," *European Judaism* 40, no. 2 (2007): 8. This article is a reproduction of a speech by Lederach. A more extensive treatment of his research can be found in his book *The Moral Imagination* (Oxford, UK: Oxford University Press, 1997).

[29]Nussbaum, *Cultivating Humanity*, 11.

[30]Michael J. Stoltzfus and James A. Reffel, "Cultivating an Appreciation for Diverse Religious Worldviews through Cooperative Learning in Undergraduate Classrooms," *Religious Education* 104, no. 5 (2009): 549.

[31]Eboo Patel, "Toward a Field of Interfaith Studies," *Liberal Education* 99, no. 4 (2013): 41.

[32]Detailed case studies on the topic of navigating religious diversity are also available from the following resources: "Case Study Initiative," Harvard University Pluralism Project, www.pluralism.org/casestudy#cases; "Case Studies for Exploring Interfaith Cooperation: Classroom Tools," Interfaith Youth Core, www.ifyc.org/resources/case-studies-exploring-inter faith-cooperation-classroom-tools; and Eboo Patel and Cassie Meyer, "Current Events as Interfaith Engagement Case Studies," *Teaching Theology and Religion* 16, no. 4 (2013): 390.

[33]Several research papers on this topic are available from IDEA, a nonprofit organization focusing on teaching and learning effectiveness within the context of higher education, www.ideaedu.org

[34]To inspire your writing, you might consider downloading Interfaith Youth Core's free resource "Identifying a Theology or Ethic of Interfaith Cooperation," www.ifyc.org/resources/identifying-theology-or-ethic -interfaith-cooperation. Also see Marion Larson and Sara Shady, "Love

My (Religious) Neighbor: A Pietist Approach to Christian Responsibility in a Pluralistic World," in *The Pietist Vision of Christian Higher Education*, ed. Chris Gehrz (Downers Grove, IL: Intervarsity Press, 2015), 134-48.

[35]Nussbaum, *Cultivating Humanity*, 88.

[36]Stoltzfus and Reffel, "Cultivating an Appreciation," 549.

[37]Ibid.

[38]Kunzman, "Imaginative Engagement," 526.

8 INTERFAITH ENGAGEMENT BEYOND THE BUBBLE

[1]Douglas Jacobsen and Rhonda Hustedt Jacobsen, *No Longer Invisible: Religion in University Education* (New York: Oxford University Press, 2012), 66.

[2]Alyssa N. Rockenbach et al., "Fostering the Pluralism Orientation of College Students through Interfaith Co-curricular Engagement," *Review of Higher Education* 39, no. 1 (2015): 49.

[3]Ibid.

[4]Ibid.

[5]Ibid., 51.

[6]"About the Movement," Interfaith Youth Core, accessed November 18, 2015, www.ifyc.org/about.

[7]Gustav Niebuhr, *Beyond Tolerance: Searching for Interfaith Understanding in America* (New York: Viking, 2008), xxxvi.

[8]"The President's Interfaith and Community Service Campus Challenge," Office of Faith-Based and Neighborhood Partnerships, The White House, accessed November 18, 2015, www.whitehouse.gov/administration/eop/ofbnp/interfaithservice.

[9]Eboo Patel, "Storytelling as a Key Methodology for Interfaith Work," *Journal of Ecumenical Studies* 43, no. 2 (2008): 35-46.

[10]See for example, Eboo Patel, "Is Interfaith Understanding Possible?," MPR News, Minnesota Public Radio, May 8, 2009, www.minnesota.publicradio.org/display/web/2009/05/08/midday1.

[11]Eboo Patel, *Acts of Faith* (Boston: Beacon Press, 2007), xv.

[12]"Sankofa Ojibwe and Dakota Trip," Bethel University, accessed November 18, 2015, www.bethel.edu/undergrad/campus-ministries/trips/sankofa.

[13]Ibid.

[14]David I. Smith and Barbara Carvill, *The Gift of the Stranger: Faith, Hospitality, and Foreign Language Learning* (Grand Rapids: Eerdmans, 2000), 92.

[15]Omid Safi, "The Asymmetry of Interfaith Dialogue," On Being, accessed November 20, 2015, www.onbeing.org/blog/omid-safi-the-asymmetry -of-interfaith-dialogue/8076.

[16]Ibid.

CONCLUSION: ACROSS THE BRIDGE

[1]Todd H. Green, *The Fear of Islam: An Introduction to Islamophobia in the West* (Minneapolis: Fortress Press, 2015), 9.

[2]Ibid., 103.

[3]Ibid., 327.

Index

Finding the Textbook You Need

The IVP Academic Textbook Selector
is an online tool for instantly finding the IVP books
suitable for over 250 courses across 24 disciplines.

---

ivpacademic.com
